The Little Sarasota DINING Book.

dS dineSARASOTA

2016

The Little Sarasota DINING Book.
6th Edition | 2016

To contact us, please send email to:
press@dinesarasota.com

Printed in the USA

10 9 8 7 6 5 4 3 2 1

ISBN 978-0-9862840-1-4

THANK YOU!

Thank you, thank you, thank you! Big projects like this don't just happen by themselves. It's great to work and live in a city that has so much food-centric talent. I feel lucky to have had some of them contribute their thoughts, ideas and creations to the 2016 book you're now holding.

A BIG thanks to, Kate Atkin, Fran Casciato, Nita Ettinger, Judi Gallagher, Michael Klauber, Tommy Klauber, Cooper Levey-Baker, Sean Murphy, Sol Shenker, Shannon Black, Megan Greenberg and Jamie Jalwan for all of your time, effort and expertise. It is much appreciated.

This book (and all our other editions), wouldn't be as easy to produce without Suki Hoffman. She's an artist with the red pen. Thanks for all proofing, editing and ideas.

Lastly, thanks to you for supporting our publication and our efforts to bring reliable and quality Sarasota restaurant information to our locals and visitors. We appreciate it!

Thanks for picking up a copy of the **Little Sarasota DINING Book**. We're so happy to be a part of your dining life! Seriously, we appreciate your support and hope you'll enjoy using the 2016 edition.

What's new this year? A little and a lot. We've made a few changes and added some new pages to keep you up to date on all that is food in Sarasota. First, we've made our annual TOP 50 into a handy dandy checklist (p. 6-7). That way you can keep track (or score) of your restaurant visits. Make it a 2016 goal to eat the whole list! Let us know if you do.

We've added directories of our local breweries and brew pubs (p. 28-29). That'll make it easy to figure out a place to enjoy an ice cold local brew. Included this year, is a nice neat listing of our specialty stores and markets (p. 62-63). Everything from cheese to German sausage to fresh seafood. It's all here in one easy to use place.

Looking for a little Happy Hour fun? Thankfully, we've done all of the painful research for you. "*Get Happy*" (p. 122-123) will point you to some of the best happy hours Sarasota has to offer.

There are some great features written by some of Sarasota's best culinary talents. Yes, we have some great recipes for 2016 too. Anybody for a Watermelon Mojito?

In short, you're going to just love our 2016 dining book. Keep it close, use it often. Oh, and tell a friend!

Happy Dining!

Larry Hoffman
Publisher
dineSarasota.com

2016 DINESARASOTA TOP 50

- [ ] 1   Mattison's Forty One
- [ ] 2   Libby's Cafe + Bar
- [ ] 3   Michael's On East
- [ ] 4   Turtles on Little Sarasota Bay
- [ ] 5   Cafe L'Europe
- [ ] 6   Polo Grill & Bar
- [ ] 7   Pino's
- [ ] 8   Derek's Rustic Coastal Cuisine
- [ ] 9   Sand Dollar Rooftop Restaurant
- [ ] 10   Baker & Wife
- [ ] 11   Beach Bistro
- [ ] 12   Bijou Cafe
- [ ] 13   Rosebud's Steak & Seafood
- [ ] 14   Adriatico
- [ ] 15   Fred's Market
- [ ] 16   Off The Hook Seafood Co.
- [ ] 17   The Old Salty Dog
- [ ] 18   The Table Creekside
- [ ] 19   Munchies 420 Cafe
- [ ] 20   Fleming's Prime Steakhouse
- [ ] 21   Roessler's
- [ ] 22   Yoder's Restaurant
- [ ] 23   Harry's Continental Kitchens
- [ ] 24   Tin Fish
- [ ] 25   Duval's New World Cafe
- [ ] 26   Shaner's Pizza
- [ ] 27   Barnacle Bill's Seafood
- [ ] 28   Louie's Modern
- [ ] 29   Pier 22 Restaurant

HOW TO USE THIS CHECKLIST - Like you really need an explanation for this. But, just in case here goes. Get out there and eat through our Top 50! We've made it easy for you to keep track of your culinary adventures. These are the restaurants that you've been searching for, clicking on and downloading on our dineSarasota.com website all year. So, in a way this is really *your* Top 50. And, if you flip to the back of this book, we've left you a couple of note pages for you to keep track of your favorites. Go ahead, start your own Sarasota restaurant journal.

HOW TO USE THIS BOOK

Thanks for picking up a copy of the 2016 *Little Sarasota DINING Book*. We know you're going to keep it with you every waking moment. Now that you're the proud owner of a copy, we're going to give you some helpful inside tips on how to use the guide.

First off, it's arranged in a handy alphabetical format. So, if you know the alphabet, you can use our guide. It has basic restaurant information in each listing. Name, address, phone… It also lists the restaurants website if you would like to go there for additional information.

In the outlined bar, it will tell you the neighborhood/area the location of the restaurant. The cuisine it serves and its relative expense. It's relative to Sarasota, not NYC, keep that in mind.

The hours of operation are listed too. It's nice to know when they are open.

For each place we'll also tell you what you can expect. Is it noisy or quiet? Good for kids? Maybe a late night menu. And, finally some "Insider Tips". Hey, how about that super delicious Fourteen Hour Braised Short Rib! We'll give you the heads up so you can look and order like you're a regular.

There aren't a lot of mysterious symbols that you have to reference. If you see this *, it means the restaurant has more than one location. We've listed what we consider to be the main one. The other locations are listed in the super handy cross reference in the back of the book.

Speaking of the cross reference, here's the scoop. Restaurants are listed in alphabetical order (you're good at that now). We give you basic info. Name, address, phone. Restaurants are then listed by cuisine type and then by location. So, you can easily find that perfect seafood restaurant on Longboat Key.

OK. Here's where things really get interesting. You now know where things are located and what type of food you can expect. But, let's dive in a little deeper. Let's say you're just visiting beautiful, sunny, Sarasota and you've got kids. What would be a good choice? How about celebrating a special occasion or event. Or, maybe you would just like to eat a meal and gaze longingly upon our blue waters.

That's where our specialty categories come in. Here are some things to keep in mind. First, we've hand selected these restaurants just for you. Yes, they come from our Top 200. Second, these places may not be the only ones in town that fit the description. But, we think they're among the best. Lastly, there will be controversy. Don't get riled up. Relax and enjoy cold a one. It's only a dining guide.

LIVE MUSIC – Really self-explanatory. But, the music ranges from piano bar to acoustic guitar to rock n roll. So, you may want to see who's playing the night you're going. Also, yes, there are other places in town that have live music.

CATERING – You could probably convince most restaurants to cater your twelve person dinner or throw together some to-go food for you to arrange on your own platters. The places listed here do it for REAL.

ONLINE RESERVATIONS – There's more to online reservations than OpenTable or Yelp. The restaurants listed in this section allow you to go online and reserve a dining time without picking up the phone.

EASY ON YOUR WALLET – A little perspective is in order here. Nothing in this list comes close to the McDonalds Dollar Menu (thankfully). That being said, these are some places you could go and not dip into your kids 529 plan to pay the bill. Something to keep in mind, "Easy on the wallet" depends a little on how big your billfold is.

NEW – Do I really need to explain this? I'm hoping not. These restaurants are "relatively" new. Some have been open longer than others.

SPORTS + FOOD + FUN – If the big game is on and you want to see it. Here are some places that do that well. Lots of places have a TV in the bar. These go above and beyond that. Face painting not required.

GREAT BURGERS – Start the screaming. Nothing evokes a more passionate outcry of food worship than starting a burger debate. The truth is, we don't want to do that. But, this will probably start a conversation at a minimum. Again, lots of spots serve burgers. These standout.

NICE WINE LIST – Hhhmmm… A 1990 Cabernet or a 2011 Pouilly-Fuissé? That is one tough question. No "wine in a box" here. These restaurants all have a sturdy wine list. And, usually someone to hold your hand and walk you through it.

A BEAUTIFUL WATER VIEW – Nothing says Florida like a picture perfect view of the water. And, these places have that. The food runs the gamut from bar food to fine dining.

LATER NIGHT MENU – This is not New York, it is not Miami or Chicago either. That is the context with which you should navigate this list. Notice we said "LATER" night menu and NOT "late night menu". We're a reasonably early dining town. The places listed here are open past the time when half of Sarasota is safely tucked in bed. They all might not be 1AM, but, we do have a 4:20AMer in there.

PIZZA PIE! – Let us not tussle about the quality of the Florida pie. When all is said and done, most of us love pizza in any form. And, when you want it, you WANT IT. We think these are some great places to scratch that itch.

SARASOTA FINE DINING – I hate it when people look down their nose at our upscale dining scene. We have some damn good chefs here showing off their skills every day. They should be celebrated. This list may not contain Le Bernardin, Alinea or The French Laundry. But, we have some REAL contenders.

Lastly, there is always the question, "How do these restaurants get into this book". They are selected based on their yearly popularity on dineSarasota.com. These are the restaurants that YOU are interested in. You've been searching for them on our website all year long. There are no advertisements here. So, you can't buy your way in. It's all you. This is really YOUR guide. And, I must say you have great taste!

ADRIATICO

`NEW`

6606 Superior Drive
941-922-3080
adriaticosrq.com

GULF GATE	ITALIAN	COST: $$$

HOURS: Mon-Thurs, 5PM to 9:30PM • Fri & Sat, 5PM to 10PM
CLOSED SUNDAY

INSIDER TIP: Opened in late 2014. Chef Luigi creates some delicious daily specials. Wines by the bottle or glass. You can't possibly go wrong with the seafood special.

WHAT TO EXPECT: Nice wine list • Walk In Service • Fresh Seafood

SOME BASICS

Reservations:	YES	Carry Out:	YES
Credit Cards:	YES	Delivery:	NO
Spirits:	BEER/WINE	Outdoor Dining:	NO
Parking:	LOT	Online Menu:	YES

AMORE BY ANDREA

555 Bay Isles Parkway
941-383-1111
amorerestaurantlbk.com

LONGBOAT	ITALIAN	COST: $$$

HOURS: Dinner Daily

INSIDER TIP: Recently opened by Chef Andrea Bozzolo this Italian restaurant is sure to be a quick hit. Andrea puts his unique imprint on classic Italian cuisine.

WHAT TO EXPECT: Nice wine list • Mid-Longboat Key
Upscale Italian cuisine

SOME BASICS

Reservations:	YES	Carry Out:	YES
Credit Cards:	YES	Delivery:	NO
Spirits:	BEER/WINE	Outdoor Dining:	NO
Parking:	LOT	Online Menu:	YES

ANDREA'S
2085 Siesta Drive
941-951-9200
www.andreasrestaurantsrq.com

SOUTHGATE	ITALIAN	COST: $$$

HOURS: Mon-Sat, 5PM to 10PM • Sun, 5PM to 9:30PM

INSIDER TIP: Andrea's has a great, but, fairly pricey wine list. That said, you can bring your own bottle for a $25 corkage fee. A nice option if you have a bottle or two around the house.

WHAT TO EXPECT: Nice wine list • Quite restaurant atmosphere
Upscale Italian cuisine

SOME BASICS
Reservations:	YES	Carry Out:	YES
Credit Cards:	YES	Delivery:	NO
Spirits:	BEER/WINE	Outdoor Dining:	NO
Parking:	LOT	Online Menu:	YES

ANNA MARIA OYSTER BAR
6906 14th Street W.*
941-758-7880
www.oysterbar.net

BRADENTON	SEAFOOD	COST: $$

HOURS: Sun-Thurs, 11AM to 9PM • Fri-Sat, 11AM to 10PM

INSIDER TIP: Are you just longing for some fried clam strips? They've got 'em. They might not be classic HoJo's, but, these will certainly take care of that craving.

WHAT TO EXPECT: Good for kids • Super casual dining
Great for a big group • Big menu, lots of choices

SOME BASICS
Reservations:	YES	Carry Out:	YES
Credit Cards:	YES	Delivery:	NO
Spirits:	FULL BAR	Outdoor Dining:	YES
Parking:	LOT	Online Menu:	YES

ANNA'S DELI & SANDWICH SHOP
6535 Midnight Pass Road*
941-349-4888
www.surfersandwich.com

SIESTA KEY	DELI	COST: $

HOURS: Daily, 10AM to 4PM

INSIDER TIP: The Surfer Sandwich may not quite have legendary Sarasota sandwich status. But, it's damn close. You need to try one for yourself to decide. Don't skimp on the Anna's sauce!

WHAT TO EXPECT: Great for a beach carryout • Easy on the wallet
Sandwiches • Local favorite • Good for kids

SOME BASICS
Reservations:	NONE	Carry Out:	YES
Credit Cards:	YES	Delivery:	NO
Spirits:	NO	Outdoor Dining:	NO
Parking:	LOT	Online Menu:	YES

ANTOINE'S RESTAURANT
1100 North Tuttle Avenue
941-331-1400
www.antoinessarasota.com

GRAND SLAM PZA	EUROPEAN	COST: $$$

HOURS: Mon-Sat, 5PM to 9PM

INSIDER TIP: The goat cheese salad is a home run. You also can't go wrong with any of the mussel dishes. Recently moved from their Fruitville Road location. Same great food, new space.

WHAT TO EXPECT: Nice wine list • Quiet dining • Online reservations

SOME BASICS
Reservations:	WEB/PHONE	Carry Out:	YES
Credit Cards:	YES	Delivery:	NO
Spirits:	BEER/WINE	Outdoor Dining:	YES
Parking:	LOT	Online Menu:	YES

APOLLONIA GRILL

8235 Cooper Creek Boulevard
941-359-4816
www.apolloniagrill.com

UPARK/LWR	GREEK	COST: $$

HOURS: Mon-Sat, 11M to 10PM • Sun, 4PM to 10PM

INSIDER TIP: A big, lively restaurant atmosphere. It can be a little loud. But, you can dine outside and avoid that if you need to. The gyro platter is fantastic. Get it!

WHAT TO EXPECT: Great for kids • Groups not a problem
Casual dining • Lots of parking • Happy hour

SOME BASICS

Reservations:	YES	Carry Out:	YES
Credit Cards:	YES	Delivery:	NO
Spirits:	FULL BAR	Outdoor Dining:	YES
Parking:	LOT	Online Menu:	YES

BAKER AND WIFE `NEW`

2157 Siesta Drive
941-960-1765
bakerwife.com

SOUTHGATE	AMERICAN	COST: $$

HOURS: Brunch: Tues-Sat, 11:30AM to 2:30PM
Dinner: Tues-Sat, 5PM to 9PM

INSIDER TIP: So much to choose from at this new Southgate eatery. They've got a good burger. But, the choices don't stop there. The Korean-style BBQ ribs are unique and delish!

WHAT TO EXPECT: Artisan pizza • Great daily brunch
lots of dessert choices • Open dining space

SOME BASICS

Reservations:	YES	Carry Out:	YES
Credit Cards:	YES	Delivery:	NO
Spirits:	FULL BAR	Outdoor Dining:	YES
Parking:	LOT	Online Menu:	YES

BARNACLE BILL'S SEAFOOD

1526 Main Street*
941-365-6800
www.barnaclebillsseafood.com

DOWNTOWN	SEAFOOD	COST: $$$

HOURS: Mon-Thurs, 11:30AM to 9PM • Fri-Sun, 11:30AM to 10PM
Sun, 4PM to 9PM

INSIDER TIP: Seafood, seafood and more seafood. BB's sports a huge menu of local choices. An older crowd. Lots of early dining. The seafood strudel is a knockout.

WHAT TO EXPECT: Good beer list • Early dining
Crowed during season • Fresh local seafood

SOME BASICS

Reservations:	YES	Carry Out:	YES
Credit Cards:	YES	Delivery:	NO
Spirits:	FULL BAR	Outdoor Dining:	YES
Parking:	STREET	Online Menu:	YES

BEACH BISTRO

6600 Gulf Drive N.
941-778-6444
www.beachbistro.com

HOLMES BEACH	AMERICAN	COST: $$$$

HOURS: Daily, 5:30PM to 10PM

INSIDER TIP: One of the areas premier restaurants. Famous for their bouillabaisse. Reserve early and dine on the beach. *Florida Trend Golden Spoon Hall of Fame* restaurant for a good reason.

WHAT TO EXPECT: Great for a date • Romantic • Great wine list
Fine dining • Beautiful gulf views

SOME BASICS

Reservations:	YES	Carry Out:	NO
Credit Cards:	YES	Delivery:	NO
Spirits:	FULL BAR	Outdoor Dining:	YES
Parking:	VALET	Online Menu:	YES

BIG WATER FISH MARKET

6641 Midnight Pass Road
941-554-8101
www.bigwaterfishmarket.com

SIESTA KEY	SEAFOOD	COST: $$

HOURS: Mon-Thurs, 10AM to 6:45PM • Fri, 10AM to 8PM
Sat, 10AM to 6PM • Sun, 11AM to 4PM

INSIDER TIP: Fresh fish market close by Siesta's south bridge. They feature both prepared seafood dishes and a seafood case. Like to really interact with your food? A steamer pot is for you!

WHAT TO EXPECT: Casual seafood experience • Raw bar
Steamed seafood • Ample parking • BYOB

SOME BASICS

Reservations:	NONE	Carry Out:	YES
Credit Cards:	YES	Delivery:	NO
Spirits:	BYOB	Outdoor Dining:	NO
Parking:	LOT	Online Menu:	YES

THE BEACHHOUSE RESTAURANT

200 Gulf Drive N.
941-779-2222
beachhouse.groupersandwich.com

BRADNT. BCH	AMERICAN	COST: $$

HOURS: Sun-Thurs, 11:30AM to 9PM • Fri & Sat, 11:30AM to 10PM

INSIDER TIP: Just remodeled in 2014. Lots of outdoor seating with outstanding views of the gulf. They're proud of their locally sourced ingredients. An ideal place to host an event.

WHAT TO EXPECT: Great for a date • Florida seafood • Nice wine list

SOME BASICS

Reservations:	NONE	Carry Out:	YES
Credit Cards:	YES	Delivery:	NO
Spirits:	FULL BAR	Outdoor Dining:	YES
Parking:	LOT	Online Menu:	YES

BIJOU CAFE

1287 First Street
941-366-8111
www.bijoucafe.net

DOWNTOWN	AMERICAN	COST: $$$

HOURS: Mon-Fri, 11AM to 2PM • Mon-Thurs, 5PM to 9PM
Fri & Sat, 5PM to 10PM

INSIDER TIP: One of Sarasota's best known upscale restaurants. Bijou stands for excellent service and delicious dining. Great downtown location. The shrimp piri piri always rocks!

WHAT TO EXPECT: Great for a date • Excellent wine list
OpenTable reservations • Fine dining • Happy hour

SOME BASICS

Reservations:	WEB/PHONE	Carry Out:	NO
Credit Cards:	YES	Delivery:	NO
Spirits:	FULL BAR	Outdoor Dining:	YES
Parking:	VALET	Online Menu:	YES

BLASÉ CAFE

5263 Ocean Boulevard
941-349-9822
www.theblasecafe.com

SIESTA KEY	AMERICAN	COST: $$

HOURS: Sun-Thurs, 4:30PM to 12AM • Fri-Sun, 4:30PM to 2AM

INSIDER TIP: A Siesta Village gem. Blasé offers a laid back bar scene and casual dining with a flair. A local hangout for sure. They feature specialty martinis. Start with some crab bisque.

WHAT TO EXPECT: Live music • Casual Florida dining
Local bar scene • Siesta Village

SOME BASICS

Reservations:	YES	Carry Out:	NO
Credit Cards:	YES	Delivery:	NO
Spirits:	FULL BAR	Outdoor Dining:	YES
Parking:	LOT	Online Menu:	YES

BLU KOUZINA

25 North Boulevard of Presidents
941-388-2619
blukouzina.com/US

ST ARMANDS	GREEK	COST: $$$

HOURS: Mon-Fri, 8:30AM to 3PM • Sat & Sun, 8AM to 3PM
Mon-Sun, 5PM to 9:30PM

INSIDER TIP: Upscale Greek cuisine and St. Armands atmosphere. Lots to choose from including my fav, taramosalata. A super seafood platter and great salads are featured.

WHAT TO EXPECT: Nice wine list • REAL Greek cuisine
OpenTable reservations • Many small plate appetizers

SOME BASICS

Reservations:	WEB/PHONE	Carry Out:	YES
Credit Cards:	YES	Delivery:	NO
Spirits:	BEER/WINE	Outdoor Dining:	YES
Parking:	STREET	Online Menu:	YES

BLUE ROOSTER

1525 4th Street
941-388-7539
www.blueroostersrq.com

DOWNTOWN	AMERICAN	COST: $$

HOURS: Mon & Tues, 5PM to 10PM • Wed, 5PM to 11PM
Thur, 5PM to 12AM • Fri & Sat, 5PM to 1AM • Sun, 11:30AM to 2:30PM
Sun, 5PM to 10PM

INSIDER TIP: Great fried chicken. The menu is southern comfort food and it's done right. catfish, shrimp & grits... They have fantastic live music and 16oz. PBR in a can!

WHAT TO EXPECT: Live music • Good for kids • Lively atmosphere

SOME BASICS

Reservations:	YES	Carry Out:	YES
Credit Cards:	YES	Delivery:	NO
Spirits:	FULL BAR	Outdoor Dining:	YES
Parking:	LOT/STREET	Online Menu:	YES

BOATYARD WATERFRONT BAR & GRILL

1500 Stickney Point Road
941-921-6200
www.boatyardwaterfrontgrill.com

STICKNEY PT.	AMERICAN	COST: $$

HOURS: Mon-Thurs, 11:30AM to 9PM • Fri-Sat, 11:30AM to 10PM
Sun, 12PM to 9PM

INSIDER TIP: Nice outdoor dining space with a water view.
A casual Florida dining experience. Grouper, crab & mahi are
featured prominently. You may even see a manatee float by!

WHAT TO EXPECT: Good for kids • Water view • Happy hour
Lots of parking

SOME BASICS

Reservations:	YES	Carry Out:	YES
Credit Cards:	YES	Delivery:	NO
Spirits:	FULL BAR	Outdoor Dining:	YES
Parking:	LOT	Online Menu:	YES

BONJOUR FRENCH CAFE

5214 Ocean Boulevard
941-346-0600
bonjourfrenchcafe.com

SIESTA KEY	FRENCH	COST: $$

HOURS: Daily, 7:30AM to 4PM

INSIDER TIP: A taste of Paris on Siesta Key. Fresh baguette
sandwiches. Refreshing salads. Outdoor dining right on the
Ocean Boulevard sidewalk. A European cafe experience.

WHAT TO EXPECT: Great place to meet-up • Breakfast & Lunch
Great Siesta people watching • Casual cafe

SOME BASICS

Reservations:	NONE	Carry Out:	YES
Credit Cards:	YES	Delivery:	NO
Spirits:	BEER/WINE	Outdoor Dining:	YES
Parking:	LOT/STREET	Online Menu:	YES

THE BREAKFAST HOUSE

1817 Fruitville Road
941-366-6860

DOWNTOWN	AMERICAN	COST: $$

HOURS: Mon. thru Sat., 7am to 2pm • Sunday, 9am to 2pm

INSIDER TIP: Small, quaint, downtown breakfast spot. A menu of traditional breakfast items. It's cozy and a great break from some of the places that try way too hard to be cute.

WHAT TO EXPECT: Good for kids • Breakfast/Lunch only
Easy on the wallet

SOME BASICS

Reservations:	NONE	Carry Out:	YES
Credit Cards:	YES	Delivery:	NO
Spirits:	NONE	Outdoor Dining:	YES
Parking:	LOT/STREET	Online Menu:	NO

THE BROKEN EGG

4031 Clark Road
941-922-2868
www.thebrokenegg.com

CLARK RD.	AMERICAN	COST: $$

HOURS: Daily, 7:30AM to 2:30PM

INSIDER TIP: The last remaining "original" Broken Egg. Same great menu and service. They still serve their "Incredible Hash Browns", but, they're not noted that way on their menu.

WHAT TO EXPECT: Good for kids • Breakfast & Lunch

SOME BASICS

Reservations:	NONE	Carry Out:	YES
Credit Cards:	YES	Delivery:	NO
Spirits:	BEER/WINE	Outdoor Dining:	YES
Parking:	LOT	Online Menu:	YES

BURNS COURT CAFE
401 South Pineapple Avenue
941-312-6633
www.burnscourtcafe.com

BURNS COURT	AMERICAN	COST: $$

HOURS: Mon-Sat, 8:30AM to 5PM • CLOSED SUNDAY

INSIDER TIP: I love the Burns Court area. This little eatery has that same, urban-light, neighborhood feel. Nice and cozy. Great coffee selection. Hey, try a crepe!

WHAT TO EXPECT: Casual dining • Great place to meet friends
Jazz Nights

SOME BASICS

Reservations:	NONE	Carry Out:	YES
Credit Cards:	YES	Delivery:	YES
Spirits:	BEER/WINE	Outdoor Dining:	YES
Parking:	STREET	Online Menu:	YES

CAFE DON GIOVANNI
5610 Gulf of Mexico Drive
941-383-0013

LONGBOAT KEY	ITALIAN	COST: $$

HOURS: Mon-Sat, 4:30PM to 9:30PM • CLOSED SUNDAY

INSIDER TIP: It's been on Longboat for a long time. Not much to look at on the inside. But, serving great traditional Italian dishes. Mid-LBK location.

WHAT TO EXPECT: Casual dining • Early dining crowd

SOME BASICS

Reservations:	YES	Carry Out:	YES
Credit Cards:	YES	Delivery:	NO
Spirits:	BEER/WINE	Outdoor Dining:	YES
Parking:	LOT	Online Menu:	NO

CAFE EPICURE

1298 Main Street
941-366-5648
www.cafeepicuresrq.com

DOWNTOWN	ITALIAN	COST: $$

HOURS: Mon-Sun, 11AM to 10:30PM

INSIDER TIP: The corner of Main & Palm is hot! Lots going on right there. And, Epicure is in the center of the action. Great pizzas. Outdoor dining is a must. Open late night. Gelato.

WHAT TO EXPECT: Great for a date • Pre/Post show dining
Casual Italian fare

SOME BASICS

Reservations:	YES	Carry Out:	YES
Credit Cards:	YES	Delivery:	NO
Spirits:	FULL BAR	Outdoor Dining:	YES
Parking:	STREET/PALM GARAGE	Online Menu:	YES

CAFE GABBIANO

5104 Ocean Boulevard
941-349-1423
www.cafegabbiano.com

SIESTA KEY	ITALIAN	COST: $$$

HOURS: Daily, 5PM to 10PM

INSIDER TIP: Featuring an outdoor deck for dining and enjoying a nice Sarasota evening. Great wines to choose from. The costolette di vitello is great. They serve Allen Brothers steaks.

WHAT TO EXPECT: Great wine list • Siesta Village
Nice outdoor dining space

SOME BASICS

Reservations:	WEB/PHONE	Carry Out:	YES
Credit Cards:	YES	Delivery:	NO
Spirits:	FULL BAR	Outdoor Dining:	YES
Parking:	LOT	Online Menu:	YES

CAFE IN THE PARK

2010 Adams Lane
941-361-3032
www.cafeinthepark.org

DOWNTOWN	AMERICAN	COST: $$

HOURS: Daily, 11AM to 6PM

INSIDER TIP: This unique little cafe is locate in Payne Park. Great for a casual, outdoor sandwich. A limited menu. But, what they offer is always quality. They have a Nutella pressed sandwich!

WHAT TO EXPECT: Great for outdoor lunch • Organic & local fare

SOME BASICS

Reservations:	NONE	Carry Out:	YES
Credit Cards:	YES	Delivery:	NO
Spirits:	BEER/WINE	Outdoor Dining:	YES
Parking:	LOT	Online Menu:	YES

CAFE L'EUROPE

431 St. Armands Circle
941-388-4415
www.cafeleurope.net

ST. ARMANDS	EUROPEAN	COST: $$

HOURS: Daily, 11AM to 10PM

INSIDER TIP: A St. Armands favorite since 1973. You should try the brandied duckling L'Europe. Also, the grouper margarita is a can't miss dish.

WHAT TO EXPECT: Great wine list • Catering available
Outdoor cafe style dining • St. Amands shopping

SOME BASICS

Reservations:	WEB/PHONE	Carry Out:	YES
Credit Cards:	YES	Delivery:	NO
Spirits:	FULL BAR	Outdoor Dining:	YES
Parking:	VALET/STREET	Online Menu:	YES

CAFÉ VENICE

116 W. Venice Avenue
941-484-1855
www.cafeveniceontheisland.com

VENICE	AMERICAN	COST: $$

HOURS: Mon-Sat, 11:30AM to 9PM

INSIDER TIP: Great Venice Island food find. Creative, made from scratch dishes that everyone will enjoy. A respectable beer and wine list has plenty of selections to accompany your meal.

WHAT TO EXPECT: Upscale, casual dining • Live music

SOME BASICS

Reservations:	YES	Carry Out:	YES
Credit Cards:	YES	Delivery:	NO
Spirits:	BEER/WINE	Outdoor Dining:	YES
Parking:	STREET	Online Menu:	YES

CAPTIAN BRIAN'S SEAFOOD MARKET & RESTAURANT

8421 North Tamiami Trail
941-351-4492
www.captainbriansseafood.com

NORTH TRAIL	SEAFOOD	COST: $$

HOURS: Mon-Sun, 11AM to 9PM

INSIDER TIP: This is old school, Sarasota seafood. It's an early dining crowd here. There's lots of local catches. The ambiance is plain, but, hey, you're here for the seafood anyway.

WHAT TO EXPECT: Casual • Seafood market • Good for kids

SOME BASICS

Reservations:	NONE	Carry Out:	YES
Credit Cards:	YES	Delivery:	NO
Spirits:	FULL BAR	Outdoor Dining:	NO
Parking:	LOT	Online Menu:	YES

CAPTAIN CURT'S CRAB & OYSTER BAR

1200 Old Stickney Point Road
941-349-3885
www.captaincurts.com

SIESTA KEY	SEAFOOD	COST: $$

HOURS: Lunch & Dinner Daily

INSIDER TIP: There's a lot of seafood on the menu. Crab a lot of ways. The NE clam chowder is off the charts great! Award winning. Fantastic Buffalo wings. Also, don't miss the Sniki Tiki!

WHAT TO EXPECT: Good for kids • Super casual • Lots of seafood Ohio State football HQ• Very busy during season

SOME BASICS

Reservations:	NONE	Carry Out:	YES
Credit Cards:	YES	Delivery:	NO
Spirits:	FULL BAR	Outdoor Dining:	NO
Parking:	LOT	Online Menu:	YES

CARAGIULOS

69 South Palm Avenue
941-951-0866
caragiulos.com

DOWNTOWN	ITALIAN	COST: $$

HOURS: Mon-Thurs, 11AM to 10PM • Fri, 11AM to 11PM
Sat, 5PM to 11PM • Sun, 5PM to 10PM

INSIDER TIP: A downtown casual Italian dining tradition. Everything you would expect. Lasagna and linguine with clams are both standouts. They serve good pizza too!

WHAT TO EXPECT: Casual dining • Palm Ave. gallery district Good for kids

SOME BASICS

Reservations:	YES	Carry Out:	YES
Credit Cards:	YES	Delivery:	NO
Spirits:	FULL BAR	Outdoor Dining:	YES
Parking:	STREET/VALET	Online Menu:	YES

IDIOT BOX
Why restaurants and patrons alike need to ditch their screens.

By Cooper Levey-Baker

It must have been April 18, 2013—the day my dislike for televisions in restaurants curdled into outright hatred.

My 8-year-old godson and I were indulging in an irregular habit of ours, getting together to shoot hoops then decamping for pizza. We walked into downtown Sarasota's Il Panificio, a go-to spot for simple, crisp slices. Like always, the TV was turned on and tuned to Fox News. Bad enough to broadcast the lunatic ravings of cables news to your customers, even worse when it's three days after the Boston Marathon bombing.

I only know the date was April 18 because that was the day the FBI released images of the terrorists that had been captured by surveillance cameras. The Fox anchors and producers plastered the photos all over the screen, intercut with older stills and video of the bloody bombing itself.

We ate. But as we took down our slices, my godson kept staring at the television, asking questions about what was going on. Who were those men? All I could do was gulp. Ask your mom.

TVs in restaurants don't always ruin meals, or even whole days, like they did on that evening back in 2013, but they are almost always an abomination that has no place in civilized society. There are exceptions, of course. I love watching basketball on the screens at Mandeville or the Shamrock as much as anyone. It's pathetic that sports are one of our few community rallying points, but it's a fact, and I'll never begrudge a restaurant or bar that caters to sports fans for flicking on the game.

But for restauranteurs that aren't part of the sports-industrial complex, I'd like to ask: What does hanging a TV in your dining room ever add? You can't really enjoy a movie with the sound off, and with live news, captions offer at best a rough approximation of what's being said. Is it just something to stare at to dull yourself from the world around you? That's what I suspect, because even as much as I loathe TVs in public spaces, if one happens to be on just above the shoulder of someone I'm sharing a meal with, I can't help but feel my gaze pulled toward the glowing box and away from my interlocutor. I fight the urge, but it's pointless. Science shows that for kids under 2, digital media is nothing more than a hypnotic glowing screen. I'd wager it's not all that different for supposedly grown-ass adults, too.

It's not just on restaurants to shut down their screens. Patrons have a moral obligation to do their part, too. I'm sitting in a coffee shop as I write this, enjoying the holy blessing of free Wi-Fi, but I'd never whip out an iPad or laptop at a restaurant while eating lunch. There's a time and a place for working while you eat or sip. Coffee shop? Sure. Casual breakfast spot? Go for it. Family dinner joint where you're meeting up with friends or loved ones? Put the screen away.

"The world is too much with us," William Wordsworth wrote more than two centuries ago. If things were that bad that long ago, they're abominable today. It seems as if there's no corner of the world where we can escape the glare of the media, something I'd guess many of us crave, even when the news of the day is heartwarming rather than heartrending. Truth is, it wasn't the gory imagery of Fox News that made my Panificio pizza so bitter years ago. It was the very intrusion of television into time that should be sacred: Dinnertime with someone I love.

Cooper Levey-Baker has covered food, politics, civic issues, the arts and music in Southwest Florida for a decade, and his writing has appeared in nearly every local publication. His work has won an honorable mention from the Julia Child Foundation and a Bronze Award for Best In-Depth Reporting from the Florida Magazine Association, and he was named a finalist for Best Public Service Reporting by the Florida Society of Professional Journalists. His fiction has appeared in a number of literary journals and earned him a John Ringling Fund Individual Artist Fellowship from the Arts Council of Sarasota County. His rendition of "Drunk in Love" has left karaoke audiences throughout the region bewildered.
Follow him on Twitter: @LeveyBaker.

CARMEL CAFE

8433 Cooper Creek Boulevard
941-893-5955
www.carmelcafe.com

UPARK	MEDITERRANEAN	COST: $$

HOURS: Mon-Thurs, 11:30AM to 10PM
Fri-Sat, 11:30PM to 11:30AM • Sun, 11AM to 9PM

INSIDER TIP: One of the first places in town to have an iPad ordering system. Not sure if you're food comes out better or faster. But it's fun to order! Lots of delicious small plate choices.

WHAT TO EXPECT: Shoppes @ University Center • Fun for groups
Good wine list

SOME BASICS

Reservations:	YES	Carry Out:	YES
Credit Cards:	YES	Delivery:	NO
Spirits:	FULL BAR	Outdoor Dining:	YES
Parking:	LOT	Online Menu:	YES

CASEY KEY FISH HOUSE

801 Blackburn Point Road
941-966-1901
www.caseykeyfishhouse.com

OSPREY	SEAFOOD	COST: $$

HOURS: Daily, 11:30AM to 9PM

INSIDER TIP: There is nothing like the Casey Key Fish House. Super laid back drinking and dining. This place screams, "I'm on vacation". Even if you're a local. And, the locals love it!

WHAT TO EXPECT: Vacation atmosphere • Local seafood
Water view • Old Florida feel

SOME BASICS

Reservations:	NONE	Carry Out:	YES
Credit Cards:	YES	Delivery:	NO
Spirits:	FULL BAR	Outdoor Dining:	YES
Parking:	LOT	Online Menu:	YES

C'EST LA VIE!
1553 Main Street
941-906-9575
www.cestlaviesarasota.com

DOWNTOWN	FRENCH	COST: $$

HOURS: Daily, Breakfast & Lunch

INSIDER TIP: Would you like to take a trip to a French cafe without leaving Sarasota? A quick hop downtown is all you need. The Biarritz baguette sandwich rocks! Just my opinion.

WHAT TO EXPECT: Great outdoor tables • Relaxed cafe dining

SOME BASICS

Reservations:	NONE	Carry Out:	YES
Credit Cards:	YES	Delivery:	NO
Spirits:	BEER/WINE	Outdoor Dining:	YES
Parking:	STREET	Online Menu:	YES

CHA CHA COCONUTS TROPICAL BAR
417 St. Armands Circle
941-388-3300
www.chacha-coconuts.com

ST. ARMANDS	AMERICAN	COST: $$

HOURS: Daily, Lunch & Dinner

INSIDER TIP: A fun place for a shopping break. Especially, if you've got kids with you. Casual, island style cuisine. Good service. Fuel up and then back to the shops!

WHAT TO EXPECT: Good for kids • Great outdoor tables
Bustling atmosphere

SOME BASICS

Reservations:	NONE	Carry Out:	YES
Credit Cards:	YES	Delivery:	NO
Spirits:	FULL BAR	Outdoor Dining:	YES
Parking:	STREET/LOT/VALET	Online Menu:	YES

CHUTNEY'S, ETC.

1944 Hillview Street
941-954-4444
www.chutneysetc.com

SOUTHSIDE VILLAGE	INDIAN	COST: $$

HOURS: Mon-Sat, 11:30AM to 2PM • Mon-Sat, 5:30PM to 9PM
CLOSED SUNDAY

INSIDER TIP: Locals love it! Everyone is treated like family by owners, Ash and Denise. For lunch, the feta burger is a standout. Dinner, rogan josh or Moroccan lamb shank.

WHAT TO EXPECT: Casual dining • Mediterranean/Indian cuisine
Good beer selection • Great daily specials

SOME BASICS

Reservations:	3 OR MORE	Carry Out:	YES
Credit Cards:	YES	Delivery:	NO
Spirits:	BEER/WINE	Outdoor Dining:	YES
Parking:	STREET	Online Menu:	YES

CLASICO CAFE + BAR

1341 Main Street
941-957-0700
www.barclasico.com

DOWNTOWN	ITALIAN	COST: $$

HOURS: Sun-Wed, 11:30AM to 1AM • Thurs-Sat, 11:30M to 2AM

INSIDER TIP: Part of the new hot corner downtown. Main and Palm is hopping and Clasico is right there. Lunch? The Clasico hot Sicilian sandwich is hard to beat.

WHAT TO EXPECT: Great for a date • Live music • Energetic scene

SOME BASICS

Reservations:	YES	Carry Out:	YES
Credit Cards:	YES	Delivery:	NO
Spirits:	FULL BAR	Outdoor Dining:	YES
Parking:	STREET/PALM GARAGE	Online Menu:	YES

CLAYTON'S SIESTA GRILLE

1256 Old Stickney Point Road
941-349-2800
www.claytonssiestagrille.com

SIESTA KEY	AMERICAN	COST: $$

HOURS: Mon-Tues, 4PM to 10PM • Wed & Thurs, 8AM to 10PM
Fri & Sat, 8AM to 10:30PM • Sun, 8AM to 10PM

INSIDER TIP: Right off the Stickney Point bridge. A great stop for breakfast on the way to the beach. Or, an early after beach dinner. Nice outdoor seating space.

WHAT TO EXPECT: Casual dining • Siesta south bridge

SOME BASICS

Reservations:	YES	Carry Out:	YES
Credit Cards:	YES	Delivery:	YES
Spirits:	FULL BAR	Outdoor Dining:	YES
Parking:	LOT	Online Menu:	YES

COFFEE CARROUSEL

1644 Main Street
941-365-2826

DOWNTOWN	AMERICAN	COST: $

HOURS: Mon-Sat, 6AM to 2PM

INSIDER TIP: Downtown tradition. Make no mistake, this is a coffee shop. Counter stool and all. Before Facebook, this is where you did your local social networking! Probably still can.

WHAT TO EXPECT: Diner experience • All locals • Good service
Cheap eats

SOME BASICS

Reservations:	NONE	Carry Out:	YES
Credit Cards:	YES	Delivery:	NO
Spirits:	NONE	Outdoor Dining:	NO
Parking:	STREET	Online Menu:	NO

THE COLUMBIA RESTAURANT
411 St. Armands Circle
941-388-3987
www.columbiarestaurant.com

ST. ARMANDS	CUBAN	COST: $$

HOURS: Sun-Thurs, 11AM to 10PM • Fri & Sat, 11AM to 11PM

INSIDER TIP: The "Gem of Spanish Restaurants". And, it is! A St. Armands tradition for locals and visitors. The 1905 Salad is mandatory. Soup, salad & sandwich combos for lunch.

WHAT TO EXPECT: Fantastic sangria • Excellent service
OpenTable reservations • Very busy in season

SOME BASICS

Reservations:	WEB/PHONE	Carry Out:	YES
Credit Cards:	YES	Delivery:	NO
Spirits:	FULL BAR	Outdoor Dining:	YES
Parking:	STREET/LOT/VALET	Online Menu:	YES

CORKSCREW DELI
4982 South Tamiami Trail
941-925-3955
www.corkscrewdeli.com

SOUTH TRAIL	DELI	COST: $

HOURS: Mon-Sat, 10AM to 5PM • CLOSED SUNDAY

INSIDER TIP: It's not Katz or Manny's, but, you also don't have to get on a plane. Serving all Boar's Head deli products. A wide selection of sandwiches. Quick lunch service.

WHAT TO EXPECT: Easy on the wallet • Quick lunch • Friendly staff

SOME BASICS

Reservations:	NONE	Carry Out:	YES
Credit Cards:	YES	Delivery:	YES
Spirits:	NONE	Outdoor Dining:	YES
Parking:	LOT	Online Menu:	YES

COSIMO'S TRATTORIA & BAR
3501 Palmer Crossing Circle
941-922-7999
www.cosimos.net

CLARK RD	ITALIAN	COST: $$

HOURS: Mon-Thurs, 11:30AM to 9:30PM
Fri & Sat, 11:30AM to 10:30PM • Sun, Noon to 9PM

INSIDER TIP: I'll be honest. I miss the old pizza by the slice at the Southgate Mall. Thankfully, you can still get their award winning quattro formaggio pizza at the new location.

WHAT TO EXPECT: Casual dining • Reservation & call ahead

SOME BASICS

Reservations:	YES	Carry Out:	YES
Credit Cards:	YES	Delivery:	NO
Spirits:	FULL BAR	Outdoor Dining:	YES
Parking:	LOT	Online Menu:	YES

THE COTTAGE
153 Avenida Messina
941-312-9300
www.cottagesiestakey.com

SIESTA KEY	AMERICAN	COST: $$

HOURS: Daily, 11AM to 10PM

INSIDER TIP: In Siesta Village. Small and large plate dishes. The building resembles a wooden cottage. It's a great place to meet-up for a drink before strolling the village.

WHAT TO EXPECT: Tapas • Siesta Village • Outdoor dining

SOME BASICS

Reservations:	NONE	Carry Out:	YES
Credit Cards:	YES	Delivery:	NO
Spirits:	FULL BAR	Outdoor Dining:	YES
Parking:	STREET/VALET	Online Menu:	YES

CRAB & FIN

420 St. Armands Circle
941-388-3964
crabfinrestaurant.com

ST. ARMANDS	SEAFOOD	COST: $$$

HOURS: Sun-Thurs, 11:30AM to 10PM
Fri & Sat, 11:30AM to 10:30PM

INSIDER TIP: White table cloth dining. Great, fresh local seafood. They've been on the circle since 1978. They must be doing something right. A big selection of oysters.

WHAT TO EXPECT: Great for a date • Good wine list
Unique seafood selections

SOME BASICS

Reservations:	YES	Carry Out:	YES
Credit Cards:	YES	Delivery:	NO
Spirits:	FULL BAR	Outdoor Dining:	YES
Parking:	STREET/LOT	Online Menu:	YES

THE CROW'S NEST

1968 Tarpon Center Drive
941-484-9551
www.crowsnest-venice.com

VENICE	SEAFOOD	COST: $$

HOURS: Mon-Wed, 11:30AM to 10PM • Thurs, 11:30AM to 11PM
Fri & Sat, 11:30AM to 12AM • Sun, Noon to 9PM

INSIDER TIP: One of Venice's premier places to dine. Great food, great views. Lots of local seafood to choose from. The Crow's Nest bouillabaisse is an excellent pick.

WHAT TO EXPECT: Water view • Good wine list

SOME BASICS

Reservations:	YES	Carry Out:	YES
Credit Cards:	YES	Delivery:	NO
Spirits:	FULL BAR	Outdoor Dining:	YES
Parking:	LOT	Online Menu:	YES

CURRENTS
1000 Boulevard of the Arts
941-953-1234

NORTH TRAIL	AMERICAN	COST: $$$

HOURS: Daily, 6:30am to 10PM

INSIDER TIP: Located in the Sarasota Hyatt, Currents delivers high quality, locally sourced dishes. Chef Kory Foltz does a nice job of making a typical hotel dining experience extraordinary.

WHAT TO EXPECT: Online reservations • Banquet facilities
Water view • Good wine list

SOME BASICS
Reservations:	YES	Carry Out:	YES
Credit Cards:	YES	Delivery:	NO
Spirits:	FULL BAR	Outdoor Dining:	YES
Parking:	LOT/VALET	Online Menu:	YES

CURRY STATION   `NEW`
1303 North Washington Boulevard*
941-312-6264
www.currystation.net

DOWNTOWN	INDIAN	COST: $$

HOURS: Lunch Buffet: Mon-Sat, 11:30AM to 2:40PM
Dinner: Mon-Sat, 5:30PM to 9PM • CLOSED SUNDAY

INSIDER TIP: They advertise "Authentic Indian" and admittedly it's pretty good. Lots of good stuff on the lunch buffet. Lots & lots & lots of choices. The lamb rogan josh stands out.

WHAT TO EXPECT: Huge Indian menu • Curry dishes featured
A dozen naan and other breads • Vegan selections

SOME BASICS
Reservations:	YES	Carry Out:	YES
Credit Cards:	YES	Delivery:	NO
Spirits:	BEER/WINE	Outdoor Dining:	NO
Parking:	LOT	Online Menu:	YES

Ahi Tuna Tartar Wonton Taco's
with Wasabi Caviar and Sakimole

Polo Grill & Bar, Chef Tommy Klauber

INGREDIENTS
1 lb sashimi grade Ahi tuna, finely diced
1/4 tsp sesame seeds, toasted lightly
1/2 tsp fresh chopped ginger
1/8 cup soy sauce
1/8 cup sesame oil
1/4 tsp black sesame seeds
32 wonton wrappers
Place tuna, marinade and sesame seeds in mixing bowl. Stir and let marinate for 5 minutes. Chill before using.

INGREDIENTS
Sakimole
2 ripe avocados, peeled and pitted
3 tablespoons peeled, seeded and small diced tomatoes
1 small jalapeño, seeded and minced
2 tbsp finely chopped onions
1 tsp minced garlic
Juice of one lemon
Juice of one lime
2 tbsp finely chopped cilantro
2 tbsp Sake
Crystal hot sauce to taste
Salt and pepper

METHOD
In a mixing bowl, mash the avocados with a fork until the avocados are somewhat mashed but still chunky. Fold in the remaining ingredients. Season with salt and pepper.

TIP: For storing: Cover tightly by layering a sheet of plastic wrap directly on the surface of the guacamole and gently squeezing out any air bubbles. Will keep for up to 8 hours.

Place wonton wrappers in a taco tongs (available on the internet) fry until light brown and crispy. Finally, assemble the tacos.

Serves 4

Renowned chef and restauranteur, Tommy Klauber was born and raised in his family's hospitality business. He earned a degree from the Culinary Institute of America and a diploma from La Varenne's Ecole de Cuisine in Paris, France. On his own, Tommy has opened three major hospitality operations: Pattigeorge's Restaurant on Longboat Key, Fete Catering & Ballroom with his wife, Jaymie, and Polo Grill and Bar in Lakewood Ranch. The businesses reflect his diverse culinary background, global influences and his commitment to fresh, locally sourced, sustainable food.

DAIQUIRI DECK RAW BAR

5250 Ocean Boulevard*
941-349-8697
www.daiquirideck.com

SIESTA KEY	AMERICAN	COST: $$

HOURS: Daily, 11AM to 2AM

INSIDER TIP: Now with three locations. The original "deck" on Siesta is still hopping with locals and visitors. Cool down with one of their signature frozen drinks. Can you say, Mangolada!

WHAT TO EXPECT: Great after the beach • Super casual

SOME BASICS

Reservations:	NONE	Carry Out:	YES
Credit Cards:	YES	Delivery:	NO
Spirits:	FULL BAR	Outdoor Dining:	YES
Parking:	STREET	Online Menu:	YES

DARUMA JAPANESE STEAK HOUSE

5459 Fruitville Road
941-342-6600
www.darumarestaurant.com

FRUITVILLE RD	ASIAN	COST: $$

HOURS: Daily, 5PM to 10PM

INSIDER TIP: A delicious mix of traditional sushi and entertaining teppan style table-side cooking. Their chefs put on a great show while making some tasty food. Good sushi too.

WHAT TO EXPECT: Fun date night • Good for kids

SOME BASICS

Reservations:	YES	Carry Out:	YES
Credit Cards:	YES	Delivery:	NO
Spirits:	FULL BAR	Outdoor Dining:	NO
Parking:	LOT	Online Menu:	YES

DEMETRIO'S RESTAURANT & PIZZA

4410 South Tamiami Trail
941-922-1585
www.demetriospizzeria.com

SOUTH TRAIL	ITALIAN	COST: $$

HOURS: Sun-Thurs, 11AM to 9PM • Fri-Sat, 11AM to 10PM

INSIDER TIP: Greek + Italian? Yes, and it works. A variety of menu items from both cuisine groups. And, as a bonus, a nice assortment of pizza options.

WHAT TO EXPECT: Great for groups • Pizza • Easy on the wallet
Good for kids

SOME BASICS

Reservations:	NONE	Carry Out:	YES
Credit Cards:	YES	Delivery:	YES
Spirits:	BEER/WINE	Outdoor Dining:	NO
Parking:	LOT	Online Menu:	YES

DER DUTCHMAN

3713 Bahia Vista
941-955-8007
www.dhgroup.com

PINECRAFT	AMISH	COST: $$

HOURS: Mon-Thurs, 6AM to 8PM • Fri-Sat, 6AM to 9PM
CLOSED SUNDAY

INSIDER TIP: Sarasota has some fantastic comfort food. Meatloaf, pork chops, you know what I'm talking about here. Oh, pie of course. Also, a nice little buffet for lunch and dinner.

WHAT TO EXPECT: Good for kids • Easy on the wallet
Home cooking • Great pie • Groups welcome

SOME BASICS

Reservations:	NONE	Carry Out:	YES
Credit Cards:	YES	Delivery:	NO
Spirits:	NONE	Outdoor Dining:	NO
Parking:	LOT	Online Menu:	YES

DEREK'S RUSTIC, COASTAL CUISINE

5516 Manatee Avenue
941-794-1100
www.dereks-bradenton.com

BRADENTON	AMERICAN	COST: $$$

HOURS: Mon-Fri, 11:30AM to 2PM • Mon-Fri, 5PM to 10PM

INSIDER TIP: Fantastic gumbo, shrimp and grits. Try the braised short ribs. Derek does creative and delicious things in the kitchen! Formerly located in the Rosemary District of Sarasota.

WHAT TO EXPECT: Great for a date • Creative cuisine
NOLA influence • OpenTable

SOME BASICS

Reservations:	WEB/PHONE	Carry Out:	YES
Credit Cards:	YES	Delivery:	NO
Spirits:	BEER/WINE	Outdoor Dining:	YES
Parking:	LOT	Online Menu:	YES

DOLCE ITALIA

6551 Gateway Avenue
941-921-7007
www.dolceitalia.me

GULF GATE	ITALIAN	COST: $$

HOURS: Tues-Sat, 5PM to 9PM • CLOSED SUNDAY & MONDAY

INSIDER TIP: Quaint. That's the perfect word here. A great family owned Italian restaurant. Gulf Gate is the ideal neighborhood to house this little gem of a place.

WHAT TO EXPECT: Great for a date • Good wine list
Lots of atmosphere • Treated like family

SOME BASICS

Reservations:	WEB/PHONE	Carry Out:	YES
Credit Cards:	YES	Delivery:	NO
Spirits:	BEER/WINE	Outdoor Dining:	NO
Parking:	LOT	Online Menu:	YES

DRUNKEN POET CAFE

1572 Main Street
941-955-8404
www.drunkenpoetsarasota.com

DOWNTOWN	THAI	COST: $$

HOURS: Sun-Thurs, 11AM to 10PM • Fri-Sat, 11AM to 12AM

INSIDER TIP: Tasty Thai cuisine. They also offer a pretty good sized sushi menu. If sushi isn't your thing, try the pad thai or the pad woonsen. Newly remodeled (2015) downtown space.

WHAT TO EXPECT: Casual atmosphere • Convenient downtown

SOME BASICS

Reservations:	WEB/PHONE	Carry Out:	YES
Credit Cards:	YES	Delivery:	YES
Spirits:	BEER/WINE	Outdoor Dining:	YES
Parking:	STREET	Online Menu:	YES

DRY DOCK WATERFRONT RESTAURANT

412 Gulf of Mexico Drive
941-383-0102
www.drydockwaterfrontgrill.com

LONGBOAT KEY	SEAFOOD	COST: $$

HOURS: Mon-Sat, 11AM to 9PM • Sun, 4:30PM to 9PM

INSIDER TIP: You've got to pay attention your first time there. It's back from the road and a little hidden. But, when you find it you'll be in for a treat. Super fresh and delicious local seafood.

WHAT TO EXPECT: Great water view • Local seafood • Happy hour

SOME BASICS

Reservations:	NONE	Carry Out:	YES
Credit Cards:	YES	Delivery:	NO
Spirits:	FULL BAR	Outdoor Dining:	YES
Parking:	LOT	Online Menu:	YES

DUTCH VALLEY RESTAURANT

6731 South Tamiami Trail
941-924-1770
www.dutchvalleyrestaurant.net

SOUTH TRAIL	AMERICAN	COST: $

HOURS: Daily, 7AM to 9PM

INSIDER TIP: There is something for everyones tastes on Dutch Valley's giant menu. The broasted chicken is a home run. Don't miss that. They also feature homemade soups and desserts.

WHAT TO EXPECT: Comfort food • Casual dining • Great for carryout
Good for kids • Early dining crowd

SOME BASICS

Reservations:	NONE	Carry Out:	YES
Credit Cards:	YES	Delivery:	NO
Spirits:	BEER/WINE	Outdoor Dining:	NO
Parking:	LOT	Online Menu:	YES

DUVAL'S NEW WORLD CAFE

1435 Main Street
941-312-4001
www.duvalsnewworldcafe.com

DOWNTOWN	AMERICAN	COST: $$

HOURS: Mon-Thurs, 11AM to 9PM • Fri-Sat, 1AM to 10PM
Sun, 10AM to 9PM

INSIDER TIP: Known for great fresh, local seafood. If you're looking for a Sunday brunch, this is a good one. Think lobster benedict and mimosas. Newly re-designed dining room.

WHAT TO EXPECT: Brunch • Busy atmosphere • Near Five Points

SOME BASICS

Reservations:	WEB/PHONE	Carry Out:	YES
Credit Cards:	YES	Delivery:	YES
Spirits:	FULL BAR	Outdoor Dining:	YES
Parking:	STREET	Online Menu:	YES

EAT HERE
240 Avenida Madera
941-346-7800
www.eathereflorida.com

SIESTA KEY	AMERICAN	COST: $$

HOURS: Daily, 5PM to 10PM

INSIDER TIP: Beach Bistro's Sean Murphy has a flair for excellent fare without the pretense. Eat Here is a casual food lovers delight. Great small plates. Can you say, "Seattle grilled cheese"!

WHAT TO EXPECT: Great for a date • OpenTable reservations
Handmade cocktails • Nice wine list • Good for groups

SOME BASICS

Reservations:	NONE	Carry Out:	YES
Credit Cards:	YES	Delivery:	NO
Spirits:	FULL BAR	Outdoor Dining:	YES
Parking:	LOT/VALET	Online Menu:	YES

EL GRECO MEDITERRANEAN CAFE
1592 Main Street
941-365-2234
www.elgrecocafe.com

DOWNTOWN	GREEK	COST: $$

HOURS: Mon-Sat, 11AM to 10PM • Sun, 5PM to 10PM

INSIDER TIP: OK, we don't have the same Greektown experience that Chicago or Detroit has. But, we have some great options. El Greco is one of them. Taramosalata! It's my favorite.

WHAT TO EXPECT: Great casual dining • Greek nights w/dancing
Good for kids

SOME BASICS

Reservations:	YES	Carry Out:	YES
Credit Cards:	YES	Delivery:	YES
Spirits:	BEER/WINE	Outdoor Dining:	YES
Parking:	STREET	Online Menu:	YES

EL TORO BRAVO

2720 Stickney Point Road
941-924-0006
www.eltorobravosarasota.com

STICKNEY PT	MEXICAN	COST: $

HOURS: Mon-Fri, 11AM to 2PM • Mon-Fri, 5PM to 9PM
Sat, 5PM to 9PM • CLOSED SUNDAY

INSIDER TIP: The real deal. Authentic Mexican cuisine. A great family run business. Love the #1 Monterrey combo plate. Good sangria too. The locals know and love this place!

WHAT TO EXPECT: Great for families • Super casual dining

SOME BASICS

Reservations:	WEB/PHONE	Carry Out:	YES
Credit Cards:	YES	Delivery:	NO
Spirits:	BEER/WINE	Outdoor Dining:	NO
Parking:	LOT	Online Menu:	YES

EUPHEMIA HAYE

5540 Gulf of Mexico Drive
941-383-3633
www.euphemiahaye.com

LONGBOAT KEY	AMERICAN	COST: $$$$

HOURS: Sun-Fri, 6PM to 10PM • Sat, 5:30pm to 10PM

INSIDER TIP: One of Longboat Key's best. Known for their duck and the prime peppered steak. Both are winners. Upstairs The Haye Loft is fun for dessert or a small plate dinner.

WHAT TO EXPECT: Great for a date • Large wine list • OpenTable
Classic dining experience • Good for special occasions

SOME BASICS

Reservations:	WEB/PHONE	Carry Out:	YES
Credit Cards:	YES	Delivery:	NO
Spirits:	FULL BAR	Outdoor Dining:	NO
Parking:	LOT	Online Menu:	YES

15 SOUTH RISTORANTE ENOTECA
15 South Boulevard of the Presidents
941-708-8312
www.15southristorante.com

ST ARMANDS	ITALIAN	COST: $$

HOURS: Sun-Thurs 4:30PM to 12AM • Fri-Sun, 4:30pm to 2AM

INSIDER TIP: Part Italian restaurant, part nightclub. They've got a nice selection of traditional Italian dishes. Plus, handmade pizzas. Music and dancing too!

WHAT TO EXPECT: Good wine list • Pizza • Later night menu
Live music

SOME BASICS

Reservations:	YES	Carry Out:	YES
Credit Cards:	YES	Delivery:	NO
Spirits:	FULL BAR	Outdoor Dining:	NO
Parking:	STREET	Online Menu:	YES

FAST N FRESH
8105 Cooper Creek Boulevard*
941-315-4500
www.eatfastnfresh.com

LAKEWOOD RANCH	AMERICAN	COST: $$

HOURS: Daily, 10AM to 9PM

INSIDER TIP: Looking for healthy and delicious meal options? This is a great one. Lots of fresh soup, sandwich and of course, salad choices.

WHAT TO EXPECT: Casual dining • Design your own salad

SOME BASICS

Reservations:	NONE	Carry Out:	YES
Credit Cards:	YES	Delivery:	NO
Spirits:	BEER/WINE	Outdoor Dining:	YES
Parking:	LOT	Online Menu:	YES

FLAVIO'S BRICK OVEN AND BAR

5239 Ocean Boulevard
941-349-0995
www.flaviosbrickovenandbar.com

SIESTA KEY	ITALIAN	COST: $$

HOURS: Sun-Thurs, 4PM to 10PM • Fri-Sat, 4PM to 11PM

INSIDER TIP: Great brick oven pizza and outstanding Italian cuisine. Name was changed From *Bella Roma Ristorante* in the past few years. But, the same great food and service

WHAT TO EXPECT: Homemade Italian cuisine • Brick oven pizza
Adult bar scene • Siesta Village location

SOME BASICS

Reservations:	YES	Carry Out:	YES
Credit Cards:	YES	Delivery:	NO
Spirits:	FULL BAR	Outdoor Dining:	YES
Parking:	LOT	Online Menu:	YES

FLEMING'S PRIME STEAKHOUSE & WINE BAR

2001 Siesta Drive
941-358-9463
www.flemingssteakhouse.com

SOUTHGATE	STEAKHOUSE	COST: $$$$

HOURS: Mon-Thurs, 4PM to 10PM • Fri-Sat, 4PM to 11PM
Sun, 4PM to 9PM

INSIDER TIP: There are a few places to eat a steak in Sarasota. This is at the top of the list. A big city steakhouse experience. Fantastic wine list. Don't forget the Fleming's potatoes.

WHAT TO EXPECT: Great for a date • Excellent wine list
Happy hour specials • Adult bar scene

SOME BASICS

Reservations:	WEB/PHONE	Carry Out:	YES
Credit Cards:	YES	Delivery:	NO
Spirits:	FULL BAR	Outdoor Dining:	NO
Parking:	VALET	Online Menu:	YES

FRESH START CAFE

630 South Orange Avenue
941-373-1242
www.freshstartcafesrq.com

DOWNTOWN	AMERICAN	COST: $$

HOURS: Daily, 8:30AM to 3PM

INSIDER TIP: Quaint local breakfast and lunch spot. Good frittatas and tons of salad options for lunch. A nice place for a casual and easy breakfast or lunch meet-up.

WHAT TO EXPECT: Casual dining experience • Sandwiches
Good service

SOME BASICS

Reservations:	NONE	Carry Out:	YES
Credit Cards:	YES	Delivery:	NO
Spirits:	BEER/WINE	Outdoor Dining:	YES
Parking:	LOT/STREET	Online Menu:	YES

GECKO'S GRILL & PUB

4870 South Tamiami Trail*
941-923-8896
www.geckosgrill.com

LANDINGS	AMERICAN	COST: $$

HOURS: Sun-Thurs, 11AM to 12AM • Fri-Sat, 11AM to 1AM

INSIDER TIP: Multiple locations. This is a great place to catch a game and enjoy some fantastic casual cuisine. Always good service. An energetic atmosphere.

WHAT TO EXPECT: Great to watch a game • Good beer list • Fun
Good burgers • Trivia nights • Florida State football

SOME BASICS

Reservations:	NONE	Carry Out:	YES
Credit Cards:	YES	Delivery:	NO
Spirits:	FULL BAR	Outdoor Dining:	YES
Parking:	LOT	Online Menu:	YES

SUNCOAST DINING, ALL THE DETAILS...
By Chef Judi Gallagher

Well, modernizing downtown seems to be the theme this year as the long awaited construction of a roundabout and the remodeling of several locations will bring mid-downtown alive again.

An all-time favorite, **Pho Cali** reopens to a new look. But, the menu still includes that same #79 with grilled pork that we have been waiting for.

Drunken Poet and **Melange** will both have a new look too. Yes, there is now a bowling alley next to them if you would like to throw a few strikes and have a cold beer.

Perhaps some of the biggest restaurant buzz this year is that we are finally getting a real New York deli. **Sol Meyer's NY Delicatessen** is so the real deal. Their pastrami and smoked white fish is coming straight from NYC. Now, I don't want to hear anyone complain that they have to pay a little more for a bigger, better real New York pastrami sandwich. It is not exactly NY prices, but the quality will be wonderful. They'll also feature fantastic potato knishes and noodle kugel. Watch out Carnegie Deli, Chef Sol may beat you in the race for the best cheesecake ever!

Back over at University Parkway, the boom continues. **Daily Eats** is coming and it is everything you want from a real diner but with a hipper vibe and healthy, hearty options. If you haven't been to the original in Tampa, you must give the new, family friendly restaurant your undivided attention. Their breakfast bowls, salad bowls, $2 mimosa happy hour and mid-afternoon burger special is a good deal! Trending across the country are home-spun shakes, breakfast all day, real homemade smoked salmon benedict and whole wheat pancakes. Mimosas and crunchy French toast round out some of Daily Eats breakfast assortment. Lunch and dinner also offer great, seasonal menu options. Best of all, their service is really good. (Something that is of high value these days.)

Eggs-TRAordinary, the breakfast and lunch café from Nokomis, has opened a second location on Cattleman next to Burlington Coat Factory. The house-made corned beef for the Reuben sandwich is just outstanding and worth the ride.

The new seasonal menu selections at **The Table Creekside** could be the best seasonal menu yet. Global is the key at this outstanding restaurant that continues to win awards. New dishes include suckling pig, branzino with romesco sauce and kelp pasta as well as a delicious Vietnamese pho with Korean short rib. They feature some new cocktails too! An Applewood infused honey bourbon poured over an orange zest ice ball has to be tasted to be believed. Add into this, the amazing water view, and boom!

Is a wonderful waterfront grouper sandwich or sushi on your mind? The new owners of **Blu Mangrove Grill** have changed the place completely. Fresh seafood and local clams, stone crabs, sushi and the best black grouper sandwich I have had to date! Located in Palmetto at Riviera Dunes, which is just over the bridge from Manatee, This is great spot to play tourist and enjoy one of the best deals yet, twin Maine lobsters every Wednesday night for $24.00. AHHHH this is Suncoast living and dining!

Curry Station has opened a second location on Clark Road. A darn good lunch buffet, (and I don't even like buffets) while their expansive dinner menu offers tandoor, goat, curry lamb and fabulous vegetable samosas. It is good, really good. The naan bread is freshly cooked in their tandoor oven.

Our favorite little sweet bakery, **SIFT** at 1383 McAnsh Square, Sarasota continues to delight our sweet tooth with apple crisp, a grandma's buttermilk cake and morning glory muffins that are just divine.

While there are more restaurants to come and never enough pages to list all my favorite dishes or the places with the best service, you can catch my reviews on *www.sarasotamagazine. com/foodiesnotebook* and the best of segments on ABC 7 every Wednesday on The Suncoast View.

Judi Gallagher is the Culinary Director for WWSB ABC 7. Her daily inspired cooking shows appear at noon. Judi is also the contributing food and wine editor of Sarasota Magazine as well as co-publisher of www.mycookingmagazine.com. Judi's outreach with community, non-profits and passion for helping children learn to cook has earned her numerous awards. Judi Gallagher is also the President of Judi Gallagher & Associates a national Hospitality Public Relations Firm.

GENTILE BROTHERS CHEESESTEAKS
7523 South Tamiami Trail
941-926-0441
www.gentilesteaks.com

SOUTH TRAIL	AMERICAN	COST: $

HOURS: Mon-Sat, 11AM to 7PM • CLOSED SUNDAY

INSIDER TIP: If I was from Philly, I would be there four times a week! It's the real deal. Amoroso bread. Cheese Whiz, of course. Tender, delicious, Philly steak sandwiches!

WHAT TO EXPECT: Philly experience • No frills dining
Easy on the wallet • Family owned • Good for kids

SOME BASICS

Reservations:	NONE	Carry Out:	YES
Credit Cards:	YES	Delivery:	YES
Spirits:	NONE	Outdoor Dining:	NO
Parking:	LOT	Online Menu:	YES

GILLIGAN'S ISLAND BAR

5253 Ocean Boulevard
941-346-8122
www.gilligansislandbar.com

SIESTA KEY	AMERICAN	COST: $$

HOURS: Mon-Sat, 11AM to 2:15AM • Sun, 12PM to 2:15AM

INSIDER TIP: Siesta Key casual. Gilligan's has live music and a lively crowd. Busy during season. But, that's the fun of it. Locals and visitors hangout here. New tiki roof adds to the atmosphere.

WHAT TO EXPECT: Siesta Village • Live music • Younger crowd

SOME BASICS

Reservations:	NONE	Carry Out:	YES
Credit Cards:	YES	Delivery:	NO
Spirits:	FULL BAR	Outdoor Dining:	YES
Parking:	STREET	Online Menu:	YES

THE GRASSHOPPER

7253 South Tamiami Trail
941-923-3688
thegrasshoppertexmex.com

SOUTH TRAIL	MEXICAN	COST: $

HOURS: Mon-Thurs, 11AM to 10PM • Fri-Sat, 11AM to 11PM
Sun, 4PM to 9PM • Happy Hour, 4pm to 7PM

INSIDER TIP: Great Mexican cuisine for not a lot of money. They offer a lot of choices. Margarita Monday's. A good Happy Hour. Try, mole chalupa, chile relleno & homemade tamales.

WHAT TO EXPECT: Easy on the wallet • Happy Hour
Good cocktail selection

SOME BASICS

Reservations:	YES	Carry Out:	YES
Credit Cards:	YES	Delivery:	NO
Spirits:	FULL BAR	Outdoor Dining:	NO
Parking:	LOT	Online Menu:	YES

HALF SHELL SEAFOOD HOUSE

5231 University Parkway
941-952-9400
www.halfshelloysterhouse.com

UPARK	SEAFOOD	COST: $$

HOURS: Mon-Thurs, 11AM to 10PM • Fri-Sat, 11AM to 11PM
Sun, 11AM to 9PM

INSIDER TIP: Tons of oysters plus a whole lot more. New location is in UPARK. You should really try the cinnamon roll bread pudding for dessert! Also, delicious gumbo.

WHAT TO EXPECT: Casual dining • Good for kids • Local seafood

SOME BASICS

Reservations:	YES	Carry Out:	YES
Credit Cards:	YES	Delivery:	NO
Spirits:	FULL BAR	Outdoor Dining:	NO
Parking:	LOT	Online Menu:	YES

HARRY'S CONTINENTAL KITCHENS

525 St. Judes Drive
941-383-0777
www.harryskitchen.com

LONGBOAT KEY	AMERICAN	COST: $$$

HOURS: Tues-Sun, 9AM to 9PM • CLOSED MONDAY

INSIDER TIP: Harry's is a Longboat tradition. Not only is the restaurant great. But, the deli is not to be missed. They are usually running a special. Their website has details.

WHAT TO EXPECT: Great for a date • Specials • Longboat Key
Info packed email newsletter

SOME BASICS

Reservations:	YES	Carry Out:	YES
Credit Cards:	YES	Delivery:	NO
Spirits:	FULL BAR	Outdoor Dining:	YES
Parking:	LOT	Online Menu:	YES

HEAVEN HAM & DEVIL DOGS

2647 Mall Drive
941-923-2514
hamheavenanddevildogs.webs.com

GULF GATE	DELI	COST: $

HOURS: Mon-Sat, 11AM to 3AM • CLOSED SUNDAY

INSIDER TIP: They actually boast the "Best Reuben in Florida". That's a HUGE statement. In all honesty, it's pretty damn good! Not much to look at on the inside. But, good eats!

WHAT TO EXPECT: Sandwiches • Easy on the wallet • Family run

SOME BASICS

Reservations:	NONE	Carry Out:	YES
Credit Cards:	YES	Delivery:	NO
Spirits:	NONE	Outdoor Dining:	NO
Parking:	LOT	Online Menu:	YES

HILLVIEW GRILL

1920 Hillview Street
941-952-0045
www.hillviewgrill.com

SOUTHSIDE VILLAGE	AMERICAN	COST: $$

HOURS: Mon-Tues, 11:30AM to 9PM • Wed-Fri, 11:30AM to 10PM
Sat, 4:30PM to 10PM • Sun, 4:30PM to 9PM

INSIDER TIP: Serves a good burger. Diverse menu. Lots of choices for everyone. Southside is a busy place these days. Hillview Grill is no exception. Nice for lunch.

WHAT TO EXPECT: Upbeat atmosphere • Large group space

SOME BASICS

Reservations:	YES	Carry Out:	YES
Credit Cards:	YES	Delivery:	NO
Spirits:	FULL BAR	Outdoor Dining:	YES
Parking:	STREET/VALET	Online Menu:	YES

HOB NOB DRIVE-IN RESTAURANT

1701 North Washington Boulevard (301 & 17th St.)
941-955-5001
www.hobnobdrivein.com

DOWNTOWN	AMERICAN	COST: $

HOURS: Sun-Thurs, 7AM to 8:30PM • Fri-Sat, 7AM to 9PM

INSIDER TIP: It's one of Sarasota best burgers. There may be debate in town about who is actually #1. But, the Hob Nob makes the top three of every list. Vintage Sarasota experience!

WHAT TO EXPECT: Easy on the wallet • Fun! • Great for kids

SOME BASICS

Reservations:	NONE	Carry Out:	YES
Credit Cards:	YES	Delivery:	NO
Spirits:	BEER/WINE	Outdoor Dining:	YES
Parking:	LOT	Online Menu:	YES

HOT DIGGITY DOG

5666 Swift Road
941-922-8018
www.theoriginalhotdiggitydog.com

AMERICAN	COST: $

HOURS: Mon, 10AM to 3PM • Tue-Fri, 10AM to 7PM
Sat, 10AM to 2PM • CLOSED SUNDAY

INSIDER TIP: Hot dog shack. One of Sarasota's oldest and best! They've been serving up a large assortment of dogs since 1970. It's certainly not fancy. But, if you want a hot dog this is it.

WHAT TO EXPECT: Easy on the wallet • Super casual
Good for a quick lunch or dinner • Good for kids

SOME BASICS

Reservations:	NONE	Carry Out:	YES
Credit Cards:	YES	Delivery:	NO
Spirits:	BEER	Outdoor Dining:	NO
Parking:	LOT	Online Menu:	YES

THE HUB BAJA GRILL
5148 Ocean Boulevard
941-349-6800
www.thehubsiestakey.com

SIESTA KEY	AMERICAN	COST: $$

HOURS: Mon-Fri, 11AM to 10PM • Sat & Sun, 11AM to 12AM

INSIDER TIP: In Siesta Village at the main intersection. It's hard to miss the hub. Big outdoor dining area and live music. It's island atmosphere for sure. Try a Hub Cuban sandwich.

WHAT TO EXPECT: Island dining experience • Good for families
Busy in season • Live music daily

SOME BASICS

Reservations:	NO	Carry Out:	YES
Credit Cards:	YES	Delivery:	NO
Spirits:	FULL BAR	Outdoor Dining:	YES
Parking:	STREET	Online Menu:	YES

HYDE PARK STEAKHOUSE
35 South Lemon Avenue
941-366-7781
www.hydeparkrestaurants.com

DOWNTOWN	STEAKHOUSE	COST: $$$

HOURS: Mon-Thurs, 5PM to 9:30PM • Fri-Sat, 5PM to 10PM
Sun, 5PM to 9PM

INSIDER TIP: Downtown Sarasota's only real steakhouse. It's got that "big city" feel to it. I'm sure you know what I mean by that. Great wedge salad. Also, lobster mac & cheese side.

WHAT TO EXPECT: Great for a date • Nice wine list • Happy hour
Good after work meet-up • Valet

SOME BASICS

Reservations:	YES	Carry Out:	YES
Credit Cards:	YES	Delivery:	NO
Spirits:	FULL BAR	Outdoor Dining:	NO
Parking:	VALET/STREET	Online Menu:	YES

IL PANIFICIO

1703 Main Street*
941-366-5570
www.panificiousa.com

DOWNTOWN	ITALIAN	COST: $$

HOURS: Tue-Sat, 9AM to 9PM • Sun & Mon, 9AM to 8PM

INSIDER TIP: Famous for downtown pizza by the slice. One of the best pizza places in town for that. Try the meatball parm sub. Also, great, fresh baked bread.

WHAT TO EXPECT: Great for lunch • Easy on the wallet • Quick
Good for kids

SOME BASICS

Reservations:	NONE	Carry Out:	YES
Credit Cards:	YES	Delivery:	NO
Spirits:	BEER/WINE	Outdoor Dining:	YES
Parking:	STREET	Online Menu:	YES

INDIGENOUS RESTAURANT

239 South Links Avenue
941-706-4740
www.indigenoussarasota.com

TOWLES CT	AMERICAN	COST: $$$

HOURS: Tue-Sat, 5:30PM to 9PM • CLOSED SUNDAY & MONDAY

INSIDER TIP: Chef Steve Phelps is one of Sarasota's best. A James Beard award nominee. Daily "Hook to Fork" specials. Plus, they serve a killer burger. Put Indigenous on your to-do list.

WHAT TO EXPECT: Great for a date • Fine dining, casual feel
Towles Court neighborhood

SOME BASICS

Reservations:	YES	Carry Out:	YES
Credit Cards:	YES	Delivery:	NO
Spirits:	BEER/WINE	Outdoor Dining:	YES
Parking:	LOT/STREET	Online Menu:	YES

JACK DUSTY

1111 Ritz-Carlton Drive
941-309-2266
jackdusty.com

DOWNTOWN	SEAFOOD	COST: $$$

HOURS: Sun-Thurs, 6AM to 10PM • Fri & Sat, 6AM to 11PM

INSIDER TIP: What you would expect from a Ritz-Carlton restaurant. Top notch Ritz service and great food. It's pricey, but, you're at the Ritz. Dine outdoors for stunning water views.

WHAT TO EXPECT: Walking distance to downtown • Water view
Handmade cocktails • OpenTable reservations

SOME BASICS

Reservations:	WEB/PHONE	Carry Out:	YES
Credit Cards:	YES	Delivery:	NO
Spirits:	FULL BAR	Outdoor Dining:	YES
Parking:	VALET	Online Menu:	YES

JOEY D'S CHICAGO STYLE EATERY

3811 Kenny Drive
941-378-8900
www.joeydspizzasarasota.com

BEE RIDGE	AMERICAN	COST: $$

HOURS: Sun-Thurs, 11AM to 10PM • Fri & Sat, 11AM to 11PM

INSIDER TIP: You get it from the name. It's Chicago. Pizza, Chicago beefs and Vienna hot dogs. Stocked with Windy City sports stuff. If you're from Chicago you'll get your "up north" fix.

WHAT TO EXPECT: Chicago food • Good for a game • Just off I-75
Good for kids

SOME BASICS

Reservations:	NONE	Carry Out:	YES
Credit Cards:	YES	Delivery:	YES
Spirits:	BEER/WINE	Outdoor Dining:	NO
Parking:	LOT	Online Menu:	YES

JOTO JAPANESE RESTAURANT
5218 Ocean Boulevard
941-346-8366
www.jotosiestakey.com

SIESTA KEY	JAPANESE	COST: $$

HOURS: Sun-Thurs, 5PM to 10PM • Fri & Sat, 5PM to 10:30PM

INSIDER TIP: Sushi and Teppan table-side cooking all in one convenient Siesta Key Village location. The table-side experience is great for groups and kids. Try the koganeyaki shrimp!

WHAT TO EXPECT: Fun for a date • Busy in season • Siesta Village Sushi bar • Tempura selections

SOME BASICS
Reservations:	YES	Carry Out:	YES
Credit Cards:	YES	Delivery:	NO
Spirits:	FULL BAR	Outdoor Dining:	NO
Parking:	STREET	Online Menu:	YES

JPAN RESTAURANT & SUSHI BAR
3 Paradise Plaza
941-954-5726
www.jpanrestaurant.com

PARADISE PLAZA	JAPANESE	COST: $$

HOURS: Mon-Sat, Lunch & Dinner • CLOSED SUNDAY

INSIDER TIP: One of Sarasota's best sushi places. Creative and inventive sushi dishes. Also, a full menu of Japanese cuisine including tempura and teriyaki. Good low carb sushi options.

WHAT TO EXPECT: Great for a date • Big sushi list • Just off Siesta

SOME BASICS
Reservations:	YES	Carry Out:	YES
Credit Cards:	YES	Delivery:	NO
Spirits:	BEER/WINE	Outdoor Dining:	YES
Parking:	LOT	Online Menu:	YES

KACEY'S SEAFOOD & MORE

4904 Fruitville Road
941-378-3644
www.kaceysseafood.com

FRUITVILLE RD	SEAFOOD	COST: $$

HOURS: Daily, 1AM to 9PM

INSIDER TIP: There's a lot going on here. A good variety of seafood options. Burgers and cheese steaks too. This is a casual experience that's good for kids and families.

WHAT TO EXPECT: Good for kids • Casual dining

SOME BASICS

Reservations:	NONE	Carry Out:	YES
Credit Cards:	YES	Delivery:	NO
Spirits:	BEER/WINE	Outdoor Dining:	NO
Parking:	LOT	Online Menu:	YES

KARL EHMER'S ALPINE STEAKHOUSE

4520 South Tamiami Trail
941-922-3797
alpinesteak.com

SOUTH TRAIL	AMERICAN	COST: $$

HOURS: Mon-Sat, 9AM to 9PM • CLOSED SUNDAY

INSIDER TIP: Sarasota mainstay. A stop from the Food Networks, *Diner, Drive-In's and Dives* put it on the map. Famous for their TurDucKen. Great meat market. German cuisine too.

WHAT TO EXPECT: Old Sarasota • Meat market • Home cooking German cuisine

SOME BASICS

Reservations:	NONE	Carry Out:	YES
Credit Cards:	YES	Delivery:	NO
Spirits:	FULL BAR	Outdoor Dining:	NO
Parking:	LOT	Online Menu:	YES

SARASOTA MARKETS AND SPECIALTY STORES

Artisan Cheese Company • 1310 Main St. • 951-7860
WHAT YOU CAN FIND THERE: Cheese store. Hard to find small domestic dairies. Lunch menu. Classes. Knowledgeable staff.

As Good As It Gets • 49 S. Palm Ave. • 373-1839
WHAT YOU CAN FIND THERE: Gourmet, upscale foods. Cheese, caviar & charcuterie. Good wine selection. Oils & vinegars.

Big Water Fish Market • 6641 Midnight Pass Rd. • 554-8101
WHAT YOU CAN FIND THERE: Fresh Florida fish. Great prepared seafood items. Just south of Siesta Key's south bridge.

The British Corner Shop • 2236 Gulf Gate Dr. • 346-6004
WHAT YOU CAN FIND THERE: British foods. Tea room. Sausage rolls, meat pies & Bridies. They feature an afternoon tea.

The Butcher's Block • 3242 17th St. • 955-2822
WHAT YOU CAN FIND THERE: Meat market/butcher shop. Custom cuts, Prime meats. Good wine selection. They have gift baskets.

Casa Italia • 2080 Constitution Blvd. • 924-1179
WHAT YOU CAN FIND THERE: A wide variety of hard to find ethnic items. Cheeses, deli & more. Cooking classes. Prepared foods

Geiers Sausage Kitchen • 7447 S. Tamiami Trl. • 923-3004
WHAT YOU CAN FIND THERE: Sausage & more sausage. Sarasota's best German market. Lots of smoked meats and deli items.

Karl Ehmer's Steakhouse • 4520 S. Tamiami Trl. • 922-3797
WHAT YOU CAN FIND THERE: Meat market. Skilled butchers, super helpful. Famous for Tur-duck-hen. Also, full service restaurant.

M & M European Deli • 2805 Proctor Rd. • 922-1221
WHAT YOU CAN FIND THERE: European, Hungarian & Polish grocery items. Great deli sandwiches. Borscht, goulash & pierogis.

SARASOTA MARKETS AND SPECIALTY STORES

Morton's Gourmet Market • 1924 S. Osprey Ave. • 955-9856
WHAT YOU CAN FIND THERE: Upscale gourmet food items including a large selection of cheeses and wine. Great deli & carryout.

Morton's Siesta Market • 205 Canal Rd. • 349-1474
WHAT YOU CAN FIND THERE: Everyday grocery items plus a good selection of prepared foods for lunch and dinner. Cold beer.

Piccolo Italian Market • 6518 Gateway Ave. • 923-2202
WHAT YOU CAN FIND THERE: Italian market. Pastas, sauces, homebaked bread and homemade Italian sausage. Sandwiches.

Walt's Fish Market • 4144 S. Tamiami Trl. • 921-4605
WHAT YOU CAN FIND THERE: Huge selection of fresh local fish & seafood. Stone crabs when in season. Smoked mullet spread!

KAZU 2.0
6566 Gateway Avenue
941-922-5459
www.kazus2srq.com

GULF GATE	SUSHI	COST: $$

HOURS: Mon-Sat, 4:30PM to 11:45PM • CLOSED SUNDAY

INSIDER TIP: Sushi, that's their thing. The former location in Southgate was tiny. Gulf Gate is larger so getting a table is a little easier. They serve a late night menu after 10PM.

WHAT TO EXPECT: Happy hour • Sushi • Kitchen menu available

SOME BASICS

Reservations:	NONE	Carry Out:	YES
Credit Cards:	YES	Delivery:	NO
Spirits:	BEER/WINE	Outdoor Dining:	NO
Parking:	STREET/LOT	Online Menu:	YES

KIYOSHI SUSHI

6550 Gateway Avenue
941-924-3781
www.kiyoshis.com

GULF GATE	SUSHI	COST: $$

HOURS:　Tues-Sat, 5:30PM to 10PM
CLOSED SUNDAY & MONDAY

INSIDER TIP: Chef Kiyoshi Noro is back! And, we're pretty excited. Formerly, downtown now in Gulf Gate. This area has lots of sushi options. Inventive and delicious sushi.

WHAT TO EXPECT: Traditional sushi • Casual & comfortable

SOME BASICS

Reservations:	YES	Carry Out:	YES
Credit Cards:	YES	Delivery:	NO
Spirits:	BEER/WINE	Outdoor Dining:	NO
Parking:	STREET/LOT	Online Menu:	YES

KNICK'S TAVERN & GRILL

1818 South Osprey Avenue
941-955-7761
www.knickstavernandgrill.com

SOUTHSIDE VILLAGE	AMERICAN	COST: $$

HOURS:　Mon-Fri, 11AM to 11PM • Sat, 5:30PM to 11PM
CLOSED SUNDAY

INSIDER TIP: This is more than a "Tavern & Grill". Much more. Fantastic daily specials. Great soup. And, of course delicious burgers. Oh, yeah, you can also get a beer. A local favorite.

WHAT TO EXPECT: Casual dining • Busy in season • Family owned

SOME BASICS

Reservations:	YES	Carry Out:	YES
Credit Cards:	YES	Delivery:	NO
Spirits:	BEER/WINE	Outdoor Dining:	YES
Parking:	STREET/VALET	Online Menu:	YES

KUMO JAPANESE STEAKHOUSE
5231 University Parkway*
941-355-5866
kumojapanesesteakhouse.com

UPARK	ASIAN	COST: $$

HOURS: Mon-Fri, 11AM to 10PM • Sat, 11AM to 11PM
Sun, 4PM to 10PM

INSIDER TIP: Sushi and hibachi style cooking. We have lots of sushi places in town. So you had better be on your "A Game" if you want to keep up. Good for families.

WHAT TO EXPECT: Good for families • Tableside cooking • Sushi

SOME BASICS

Reservations:	WEB/PHONE	Carry Out:	YES
Credit Cards:	YES	Delivery:	NO
Spirits:	FULL BAR	Outdoor Dining:	NO
Parking:	LOT	Online Menu:	YES

THE LAZY LOBSTER
7602 North Lockwood Ridge Road*
941-351-5515
www.sarasotalazylobster.com

NORTH SARASOTA	SEAFOOD	COST: $$

HOURS: Daily, 4PM to 9PM

INSIDER TIP: Lobster, obviously. And, lots of it. The lobster mac n cheese is worth the calories for sure. Try a lobster roll. Good prices too. An older dining crowd.

WHAT TO EXPECT: Great casual seafood • Early bird seating

SOME BASICS

Reservations:	YES	Carry Out:	YES
Credit Cards:	YES	Delivery:	NO
Spirits:	FULL BAR	Outdoor Dining:	YES
Parking:	LOT	Online Menu:	YES

dineSarasota Essentials

HOW TO SELECT THE PERFECT RESTAURANT WINE WITHOUT BREAKING THE BANK

By Michael Klauber, Michael's On East

It's hard to believe I've been carefully assembling restaurant wine programs and serving as an international wine merchant for more than 30 years. Where does the time go?! Wine buying—and helping guests discover a new wine—continues to be one of my favorite aspects of my professional career, and truly daily life! After all, a special bottle of wine, or bubbly, can help make any day and any meal a truly special occasion.

I've enjoyed the great privilege of discovering remarkable vintages and finding trusted wineries which produce quality, estate and domaine-bottled wines year-after-year by building relationships with family-owned and operated properties over the years. In fact, I have a personal relationship with the winemaker or winery owners behind more than 80% of the wines we offer in our restaurant and adjacent retail wine store.

Of course, in many cases, you may not personally know the people, history and complicated bouquet, aromas and flavor profiles behind each and every wine. When you are looking to find the perfect wine—within your given budget—I'd suggest a few tips!

SEEK ADVICE

Always remember to ask your server or a restaurant's sommelier for recommendations. By mentioning a few specific wines, varietals or flavor profiles you truly love – or tend to avoid – a restaurant's knowledgeable wine specialists are able to guide you to a great selection meeting your perceived favorites and also bringing out the flavors of your chosen cuisine.

TALK ABOUT THE *TASTES* YOU LIKE & WHAT YOU DON'T LIKE!

When talking about wines, don't just tell people what you like, be sure to share the tastes you may not care for as much, too. It's great if you can mention X, Y and Z wines which have been your favorite historically, but be descriptive about why you enjoyed those wines. Sharing a detailed narrative about your specific likes and dislikes will help your server or sommelier select a great new varietal for you to try—and love! Be "brave enough" to allow the restaurant's wine steward to select a wine pairing to perfectly accompany your favorite dish.

JUST A TASTE: WINE FLIGHTS

When dining out, you may also want to consider selecting a "flight" of wines. Of course, most restaurateurs are happy to provide you a taste of a wine or two as you make your dinner selections at the table, but you may also want to order a complete flight of wines. At Michael's On East, our wine flights offer four, 2.5 ounce pours of themed wines, from Light, Fragrant & Luscious Whites to Old World Reds Wine Flights.

EXPLORE NEW REGIONS

Use your nights out as an opportunity to explore new regions. Our family has enjoyed the opportunity to travel extensively to Italy, all of France's major regions, South Africa's Cape Winelands and Spain's La Rioja region—typically leading clients on Gulf Coast Connoisseur Club wine-buying trips! If you have a chance to pick-up a few new bottles to sample at home and continue to explore and define your personal preferences, I invite you to pick-up a rosé from Provence, sparkling from South Africa or great value Tempranillo from Spain, among more than 200 boutique wines under $20 (retail) from Michael's Wine Cellar. Sampling a few new wines or varietals at home will help you develop a greater comfort with restaurant wine lists. The process of figuring out what you love is the fun part of food and wine pairing!

Michael's On East is Sarasota's only AAA Four Diamond Award Restaurant, complete with a wine program which is recognized year-after-year by the Wine Spectator. Michael's Wine Cellar is a boutique wine and spirits store by day and private party venue by night. Store hours are Monday through Saturday, 10 a.m. – 6 p.m. To learn more about the Michael's restaurant, wine shop and catering operations, call 941-366-0007 or visit www.bestfood.com.

LELU COFFEE LOUNGE

5251 Ocean Boulevard
941-346-5358
lelucoffee.com

SIESTA KEY	AMERICAN	COST: $

HOURS: Daily, 7:30AM

INSIDER TIP: You want your caffeine, but, don't know where to go. Let's make this easy. If you're on SK, it's LeLu to the rescue. Super casual coffee sippin'. Good breakfasts too!

WHAT TO EXPECT: Casual Coffee • Nice Outdoor space
Center of Siesta Village

SOME BASICS

Reservations:	NONE	Carry Out:	YES
Credit Cards:	YES	Delivery:	NO
Spirits:	FULL BAR	Outdoor Dining:	YES
Parking:	STREET	Online Menu:	YES

LIBBY'S CAFÉ + BAR

1917 Osprey Avenue
941-487-7300
www.libbyscafebar.com

SOUTHSIDE VILLAGE	AMERICAN	COST: $$

HOURS: Lunch, Mon-Sat, 11:30AM to 10PM
Dinner, Daily, 4PM to Close • Brunch, Sun, 10:30AM

INSIDER TIP: The hub of activity in Southside Village. They serve an ever changing seasonal menu. Good Happy Hour specials. A great place to meet after work or a day out seeing the sights.

WHAT TO EXPECT: Great for a date • Seasonal menu • Happy hour
OpenTable reservations • Private room available

SOME BASICS

Reservations:	WEB/PHONE	Carry Out:	YES
Credit Cards:	YES	Delivery:	NO
Spirits:	FULL BAR	Outdoor Dining:	YES
Parking:	STREET/LOT/VALET	Online Menu:	YES

LIDO BEACH GRILLE

700 Ben Franklin Drive
941-388-2161
www.lidobeachresort.com/lido-beach-grille

LIDO KEY	AMERICAN	COST: $$

HOURS: Daily, 5PM to 10PM • Sunday Brunch, 10:30AM to 2PM

INSIDER TIP: The view! That's what you're getting here, the view. They offer a well rounded menu. But, it's the scenery that matters most here. Good Sunday brunch.

WHAT TO EXPECT: Sunday brunch • Water view
OpenTable reservations • Lido Beach Resort

SOME BASICS

Reservations:	PHONE	Carry Out:	YES
Credit Cards:	YES	Delivery:	NO
Spirits:	FULL BAR	Outdoor Dining:	NO
Parking:	LOT	Online Menu:	YES

LOBSTER POT

5157 Ocean Boulevard
941-349-2323
www.sarasotalobsterpot.com

SIESTA KEY	SEAFOOD	COST: $$

HOURS: Mon-Sat, 11:30AM to 9PM • CLOSED SUNDAY

INSIDER TIP: A New England lobster experience right in Siesta Village. Tons of great lobster dishes. The lobster bisque is out of this world! You need to have a cup of that.

WHAT TO EXPECT: Great for families • Lobster + • Siesta Village
Good for kids

SOME BASICS

Reservations:	6 OR MORE	Carry Out:	YES
Credit Cards:	YES	Delivery:	NO
Spirits:	BEER/WINE	Outdoor Dining:	YES
Parking:	VALET/STREET	Online Menu:	YES

LOLITA TARTINE

1419 5th Street
941-952-3172
lolitatartine.com

DOWNTOWN	FRENCH	COST: $$

HOURS: Tues-Thurs, 8:30AM to 9PM • Fri, 8:30AM to 9:30PM
Sat, 8AM to 9:30PM • CLOSED SUNDAY & MONDAY

INSIDER TIP: Not familiar with a tartine? These tasty open faced French sandwiches make for a super great lunch or light dinner. Bright, open restaurant downtown, north of Fruitville Rd.

WHAT TO EXPECT: Great for lunch • Rosemary District

SOME BASICS

Reservations:	YES	Carry Out:	YES
Credit Cards:	YES	Delivery:	NO
Spirits:	BEER/WINE	Outdoor Dining:	YES
Parking:	LOT	Online Menu:	YES

LOUIES MODERN

1289 North Palm Avenue
941-552-9688
www.louiesmodern.com

DOWNTOWN	AMERICAN	COST: $$$

HOURS: Coffee Bar 8AM to Close • Lunch, 11:30AM to 5PM
Dinner, 5pm to 11PM • Weekend Brunch, 10AM

INSIDER TIP: One of the places that helped start the downtown restaurant renaissance. A great place for an after work drink or get together. They host a large banquet space.

WHAT TO EXPECT: Great for a date • Lively atmosphere
Good wine list

SOME BASICS

Reservations:	WEB/PHONE	Carry Out:	YES
Credit Cards:	YES	Delivery:	NO
Spirits:	FULL BAR	Outdoor Dining:	YES
Parking:	PALM GARAGE	Online Menu:	YES

LYNCHES PUB & GRUB
19 North Boulevard of Presidents
941-388-5550
www.lynchespub.com

ST. ARMANDS	IRISH	COST: $$

HOURS: Mon-Sat, 11AM to 12AM • Sun, 12PM to 10PM

INSIDER TIP: Looking for Irish food? This place has some Irish menu staples (Cork cottage pie). If that's not your thing, how about a Rory McElroy sandwich! Fun and friendly.

WHAT TO EXPECT: Great for a casual meal • Irish pub

SOME BASICS
Reservations:	NONE	Carry Out:	YES
Credit Cards:	YES	Delivery:	NO
Spirits:	FULL BAR	Outdoor Dining:	YES
Parking:	STREET/LOT	Online Menu:	YES

MACALLISTERS GRILL & TAVERN
8110 Lakewood Main Street
941-359-2424
www.macallisters.com

LAKEWOOD RANCH	SCOTTISH	COST: $$

HOURS: Sun-Thurs, 11:30AM to 10PM • Fri-Sat., 11:30AM to 11PM

INSIDER TIP: Have you been yearning to try some traditional Scottish haggis? They've got it. But, the Scotch eggs and the braveheart burger steal the show here. Great Scotch selection.

WHAT TO EXPECT: Casual dining • Good for families

SOME BASICS
Reservations:	YES	Carry Out:	YES
Credit Cards:	YES	Delivery:	NO
Spirits:	FULL BAR	Outdoor Dining:	YES
Parking:	LOT/STREET	Online Menu:	YES

MADE

1990 Main Street
941-953-2900
maderestaurant.com

DOWNTOWN	AMERICAN	COST: $$

HOURS: Tue-Fri, Lunch & Dinner • Sat, 5PM to 12AM
Sun, 10AM to 3PM • CLOSED MONDAY

INSIDER TIP: This place has some delicious and creative menu items. Love the Shiner Bock braised short ribs. Great burgers too. Comfortable outside dining space.

WHAT TO EXPECT: Great for a date • Sunday brunch
Lively atmosphere • Nice bar scene

SOME BASICS

Reservations:	YES	Carry Out:	YES
Credit Cards:	YES	Delivery:	NO
Spirits:	FULL BAR	Outdoor Dining:	YES
Parking:	STREET/GARAGE	Online Menu:	YES

MADFISH GRILL

4059 Cattlemen Road
941-377-3474
www.madfishgrill.com

BEE RIDGE/I75	SEAFOOD	COST: $$

HOURS: Lunch & Dinner Daily

INSIDER TIP: Daily specials. Good soups. As you would expect seafood is their thing. Try the fried whole belly clam platter. Also, a large gluten free menu.

WHAT TO EXPECT: Great for casual dining • Early bird dining
Good for families

SOME BASICS

Reservations:	YES	Carry Out:	YES
Credit Cards:	YES	Delivery:	NO
Spirits:	FULL BAR	Outdoor Dining:	YES
Parking:	LOT	Online Menu:	YES

MAIN BAR SANDWICH SHOP
1944 Main Street
941-955-8733
www.themainbar.com

DOWNTOWN	DELI	COST: $

HOURS: Mon-Sat, 10AM to 4PM • CLOSED SUNDAY

INSIDER TIP: Never had a Famous Italian sandwich? Bummer. You should hustle right down to Main Bar and correct that. Lots and lots of great sandwich selections. Soups too!

WHAT TO EXPECT: Great for quick lunch • Easy on the wallet
Lively atmosphere • Fantastic service

SOME BASICS
Reservations:	NONE	Carry Out:	YES
Credit Cards:	YES	Delivery:	NO
Spirits:	BEER/WINE	Outdoor Dining:	NO
Parking:	STREET	Online Menu:	YES

MAIN STREET TRATTORIA
8131 Lakewood Main Street
941-907-1518
www.mstrattoria.com

LAKEWOOD RANCH	ITALIAN	COST: $$

HOURS: Mon-Thurs, 11:30AM to 10PM • Fri-Sat, 11:30AM to 11PM
Sun, 12PM to 9PM

INSIDER TIP: Pizza, flatbreads and traditional Italian dishes make up the menu at this Lakewood Ranch eatery. Friendly and experienced bar staff. How about dinner before the movie?

WHAT TO EXPECT: Great for a meet-up • Pizza • Good for families
Daily happy hour

SOME BASICS
Reservations:	YES	Carry Out:	YES
Credit Cards:	YES	Delivery:	NO
Spirits:	FULL BAR	Outdoor Dining:	YES
Parking:	LOT/STREET	Online Menu:	NO

MAISON BLANCHE

2605 Gulf of Mexico Drive
941-383-8088
www.maisonblancherestaurants.com

LONGBOAT KEY	FRENCH	COST: $$$$

HOURS: Tues-Sun, 5:30PM to 9:30PM • CLOSED MONDAY

INSIDER TIP: Fine dining. I mean it. One the best high end restaurants in town. James Beard nominated Chef Jose Martinez is the real deal. Prix fixe menu and ala carte choices.

WHAT TO EXPECT: Great for a date • Special occasions
Excellent service • Great wine list • Specialty desserts

SOME BASICS

Reservations:	WEB/PHONE	Carry Out:	YES
Credit Cards:	YES	Delivery:	NO
Spirits:	BEER/WINE	Outdoor Dining:	NO
Parking:	LOT	Online Menu:	YES

MANDEVILLE BEER GARDEN   NEW

428 North Lemon Avenue
941-954-8688
www.mandevillebeergarden.com

DOWNTOWN	AMERICAN	COST: $$

HOURS: Wed, Thurs & Sun, 11AM to 11PM • Fri & Sat, 11AM to 12AM
CLOSED MONDAY & TUESDAY

INSIDER TIP: Featuring some of the best brews in FL and around the USA. Over 100! Good burgers and house-made sausages. Check out the house made pork rinds with sea salt & siracha.

WHAT TO EXPECT: Beer & lots of it • Elevated brewpub fare
North downtown location • Just a cool place to hangout

SOME BASICS

Reservations:	NONE	Carry Out:	YES
Credit Cards:	YES	Delivery:	NO
Spirits:	BEER/WINE	Outdoor Dining:	YES
Parking:	LOT	Online Menu:	YES

MARCELLO'S RISTORANTE

4155 South Tamiami Trail
941-921-6794
marcellosarasota.com

SOUTH TRAIL	ITALIAN	COST: $$$

HOURS: Mon-Sat, 5PM to 10PM

INSIDER TIP: Small, intimate, Italian dining experience. Great personal service and a menu that includes a fresh catch of the day. You'll love the creative dishes that are offered.

WHAT TO EXPECT: Good wine list • Authentic Italian cuisine

SOME BASICS

Reservations:	YES	Carry Out:	YES
Credit Cards:	YES	Delivery:	NO
Spirits:	BEER/WINE	Outdoor Dining:	NO
Parking:	LOT	Online Menu:	NO

MARINA JACK'S

2 Marina Plaza
941-365-4243
www.marinajacks.com

DOWNTOWN	SEAFOOD	COST: $$

HOURS: Lunch, 11:15AM to 2PM • Dinner, 5PM to 10PM

INSIDER TIP: Classic Sarasota. Right on the water. If you're looking for that spot that screams FLORIDA, this is it. Excellent sherry & crab bisque and super fresh local seafood.

WHAT TO EXPECT: Water view • Dinner cruises • Live music
Nice wine list

SOME BASICS

Reservations:	YES	Carry Out:	YES
Credit Cards:	YES	Delivery:	NO
Spirits:	FULL BAR	Outdoor Dining:	YES
Parking:	VALET/LOT	Online Menu:	YES

BLINTZES

Sol Meyer's NY Delicatessen, Chef Sol Shenker

For Crepe

INGREDIENTS
1 egg
2 tbsp. of melted butter
½ cup of flour
¼ cup of milk

METHOD
In a medium size bowl mix the melted butter, milk, and the egg. When combined, slowly whisk in the flour until the batter is smooth.

Heat a Teflon sauté pan on medium high heat. Pour a thin layer of crêpe batter on the bottom of the pan. When the edges of the crepe start to get a little brown flip it to the other side. After both sides are lightly golden brown remove crepe from pan and set aside.

For Cheese Filling

INGREDIENTS
8 oz. cream cheese, room temperature
¼ cup raw sugar
2 tbsp. pure vanilla extract
½ tsp. lemon zest
1 egg

METHOD

In a medium size bowl mix cream cheese, sugar, vanilla extract, lemon zest and egg until smooth.
Lay your crepe down on a work surface. Spoon 2 tablespoons of cheese mix into the middle of the crêpe. Fold each side over and then roll.

Melt some butter in a sauté pan over medium high heat. Cook the crepe until golden brown.

Garnish with your favorite toppings. Enjoy!

Makes one generous serving

Sol grew up in Great Neck, Long Island and the Catskills, New York. His passion for food has been his guiding light, training at the Culinary Institute of America and working as an award winning celebrated chef at many of the world's finest hotels and restaurants. Very well known for the past fifteen years as "Chef Sol," he brings his passion for recreating and often improving the food of our ancestors, to Sarasota.

ABOUT US

Way back in April 2002 we started dineSarasota as a way to bring up to date restaurant and dining information to Sarasota locals and visitors. Our annual printed dining guides and our website, dineSarasota.com, have grown right along with the ever expanding Sarasota dining scene. Whether you're just visiting or you're a native, we're here to help you make the most of your local dining experiences.

MAR-VISTA RESTAURANT

760 Broadway Street
941-383-2391
marvista.groupersandwich.com

LONGBOAT KEY	AMERICAN	COST: $$

HOURS: Daily, 11:30AM to 10PM

INSIDER TIP: Located at the very northern edge of Longboat Key. Nice relaxed, casual atmosphere. The Bud & Old Bay shrimp bowl is a fantastic. Do yourself a favor and have it!

WHAT TO EXPECT: Great for families • Big list of specialty drinks
Water view • Old Florida feel

SOME BASICS

Reservations:	NONE	Carry Out:	YES
Credit Cards:	YES	Delivery:	NO
Spirits:	FULL BAR	Outdoor Dining:	YES
Parking:	LOT	Online Menu:	YES

MATTISON'S CITY GRILLE

1 North Lemon Avenue
941-330-0440
mattisons.com

DOWNTOWN	AMERICAN	COST: $$

HOURS: Mon-Thurs, 11AM to 11PM • Fri, 11AM to 12AM
Sat, 9:30AM to 12AM • Sun, 11AM to 10PM

INSIDER TIP: Right in the heart of downtown. All outdoor dining. It has a lively, adult bar scene. Menu includes brick oven pizzas and NY cheesecake. Live music too. Lemon & Main streets.

WHAT TO EXPECT: Great for a date • Good downtown meet-up spot
Live music • Good bartenders

SOME BASICS

Reservations:	YES	Carry Out:	YES
Credit Cards:	YES	Delivery:	NO
Spirits:	FULL BAR	Outdoor Dining:	YES
Parking:	STREET	Online Menu:	YES

MATTISON'S FORTY ONE

7275 South Tamiami Trail
941-921-3400
mattisons.com

AMERICAN	COST: $$

HOURS: Lunch Mon-Fri, 11:30AM to 2PM
Dinner Daily, 4:30PM

INSIDER TIP: We categorize this as American. But, a lot of Mediterranean influence going on here. Chef Paul Mattison is a local standout. Sophisticated dishes, priced right.

WHAT TO EXPECT: Large wine list • Brunch

SOME BASICS

Reservations:	WEB/PHONE	Carry Out:	YES
Credit Cards:	YES	Delivery:	NO
Spirits:	FULL BAR	Outdoor Dining:	NO
Parking:	LOT	Online Menu:	YES

MATTO MATTO

543 South Pineapple Avenue
941-444-7196
www.facebook.com/MattoMattoSRQ

BURNS COURT	ITALIAN	COST: $$

HOURS: Mon-Thurs, 11AM to 9PM • Fri & Sat, 11AM to 9PM
Sun, 5PM to 9PM

INSIDER TIP: This is a quaint little Italian eatery. On "the wedge" at Pineapple & Orange. Two styles of pizza. And, a menu well stocked with Italian favorites.

WHAT TO EXPECT: Pizza • Live music

SOME BASICS

Reservations:	NONE	Carry Out:	YES
Credit Cards:	YES	Delivery:	NO
Spirits:	BEER/WINE	Outdoor Dining:	YES
Parking:	STREET	Online Menu:	YES

MEDITERRANEO

1970 Main Street
941-365-4122
www.mediterraneorest.com

DOWNTOWN	ITALIAN	COST: $$

HOURS: Lunch, Mon-Fri, 11:30AM to 2:30PM
Dinner, Daily from 5:30PM

INSIDER TIP: A great place to catch a pre or post movie pizza. Directly across from the Hollywood 20. But, more than just pizza. The veal chop milanese is always a hit!

WHAT TO EXPECT: Pizza • Good wine list
OpenTable reservations

SOME BASICS

Reservations:	WEB/PHONE	Carry Out:	YES
Credit Cards:	YES	Delivery:	NO
Spirits:	FULL BAR	Outdoor Dining:	YES
Parking:	STREET/GARAGE	Online Menu:	YES

MELANGE

1568 Main Street
941-953-7111
www.melangesarasota.com

DOWNTOWN	AMERICAN	COST: $$$

HOURS: Daily, 6PM to 2AM

INSIDER TIP: They have a book in advance "Chef's Tour". If you're adventurous, it's a great night of dining. Also serving a menu of Champagne cocktails. Kids under 12 are not allowed.

WHAT TO EXPECT: Great for a date • Adult dining experience
Open late night

SOME BASICS

Reservations:	YES	Carry Out:	YES
Credit Cards:	YES	Delivery:	NO
Spirits:	FULL BAR	Outdoor Dining:	YES
Parking:	STREET	Online Menu:	YES

MI PUEBLO

8405 Tuttle Avenue*
941-359-9303
www.mipueblomexican.com

MEXICAN	**COST: $$**

HOURS: Lunch & Dinner Daily

INSIDER TIP: A Sarasota favorite for the past 15 years. They have a "Tequila of the Month". How can that be a bad thing? Big, extensive Mexican food menu.

WHAT TO EXPECT: Casual dining • Easy on the wallet

SOME BASICS

Reservations:	YES	Carry Out:	YES
Credit Cards:	YES	Delivery:	NO
Spirits:	FULL BAR	Outdoor Dining:	NO
Parking:	LOT	Online Menu:	YES

MI TIERRA RESTAURANT

1068 North Washington Boulevard
941-330-0196

DOWNTOWN	**COLUMBIAN**	**COST: $$**

HOURS: Lunch & Dinner Daily

INSIDER TIP: You've got to be a little adventurous the first time. Nothing to look at from the outside. Looks can be deceiving! Fantastic Columbian and Cuban dishes. No frills atmosphere.

WHAT TO EXPECT: Casual dining • Good service • Easy on the wallet

SOME BASICS

Reservations:	NONE	Carry Out:	YES
Credit Cards:	YES	Delivery:	NO
Spirits:	NONE	Outdoor Dining:	NO
Parking:	LOT	Online Menu:	NO

MICHAEL JOHN'S RESTAURANT

1040 Carlton Arms Boulevard
941-747-8032
michaeljohnsrestaurant.blogspot.com

BRADENTON	AMERICAN	COST: $$$

HOURS: Mon-Sat, 5PM to 10:30PM
CLOSED SUNDAY

INSIDER TIP: An American brasserie. MJ's features steaks and seafood. Casual atmosphere with an upscale menu. Lots of great starters to pick from. They serve a delicious honey baked brie.

WHAT TO EXPECT: Summer prix fixe menu night • A local favorite

SOME BASICS

Reservations:	YES	Carry Out:	YES
Credit Cards:	YES	Delivery:	NO
Spirits:	BEER/WINE	Outdoor Dining:	NO
Parking:	LOT	Online Menu:	YES

MICHAEL'S ON EAST

1212 South East Avenue
941-366-0007
www.bestfood.com

MIDTOWN PLAZA	AMERICAN	COST: $$$

HOURS: Mon-Thurs, 11:30AM to 10PM • Fri, 11:30AM to 12AM
Sat, 5:30PM to 12AM • CLOSED SUNDAY

INSIDER TIP: Delicious and creative entrées and starters. Great selection of steaks and seafood. Fine dining. Everyone should have the Michael's experience. Service ++

WHAT TO EXPECT: Nice wine list • Piano lounge • Catering
OpenTable reservations • Fine dining

SOME BASICS

Reservations:	WEB/PHONE	Carry Out:	YES
Credit Cards:	YES	Delivery:	NO
Spirits:	FULL BAR	Outdoor Dining:	NO
Parking:	VALET	Online Menu:	YES

MICHELLE'S BROWN BAG CAFÉ

1819 Main Street (City Center Building)
941-365-5858
www.michellesbrownbagcafe.com

DOWNTOWN	DELI	COST: $

HOURS: Mon-Fri, 7AM to 3PM

INSIDER TIP: Excellent sandwiches. Like no other in town. They put some combinations together that you would never dream of. And, they work! Great daily specials. Quick downtown lunches.

WHAT TO EXPECT: Great for a quick lunch • Easy on the wallet
Great lunch meet-up spot

SOME BASICS

Reservations:	NONE	Carry Out:	YES
Credit Cards:	YES	Delivery:	YES
Spirits:	BEER/WINE	Outdoor Dining:	NO
Parking:	GARAGE/STREET	Online Menu:	YES

MIGUEL'S

6631 Midnight Pass Road
941-349-4024
www.miguelsrestaurant.net

SIESTA KEY	FRENCH	COST: $$

HOURS: Dinner Daily from 5PM

INSIDER TIP: This place has a very loyal group of regulars. A nice menu of French dishes to choose from. It hosts a decidedly older crowd. Le chateaubriand bouquetière for two!

WHAT TO EXPECT: Good wine list • Quiet evening

SOME BASICS

Reservations:	YES	Carry Out:	YES
Credit Cards:	YES	Delivery:	NO
Spirits:	FULL BAR	Outdoor Dining:	NO
Parking:	LOT	Online Menu:	YES

MILLER'S ALE HOUSE

3800 Kenny Drive
941-378-8888
www.millersalehouse.com

BEE RIDGE/I75	AMERICAN	COST: $$

HOURS: Daily, 11AM to 2AM

INSIDER TIP: Sports bar first and foremost. Known locally as the "Sarasota" Ale House. A great place to watch a game or grab some "Zingers". An amped up, boneless wing.

WHAT TO EXPECT: Great for a game • Pizza • Raw bar
Good beer selection • Close to I75

SOME BASICS

Reservations:	NONE	Carry Out:	YES
Credit Cards:	YES	Delivery:	NO
Spirits:	FULL BAR	Outdoor Dining:	NO
Parking:	LOT	Online Menu:	YES

MOZAIC

1377 Main Street
941-951-6272
www.mozaicsarasota.com

DOWNTOWN	MEDITERRANEAN	COST: $$$

HOURS: Mon-Thurs, 5PM to 10PM • Fri-Sat, 5PM to 11PM
Sun, 5PM to 9PM

INSIDER TIP: Southern French and Mediterranean inspired cuisine. The dishes are super creative and always well executed. The Australian lamb rack and merguez sausage are great.

WHAT TO EXPECT: Great for a date • Good wine list • OpenTable

SOME BASICS

Reservations:	WEB/PHONE	Carry Out:	YES
Credit Cards:	YES	Delivery:	NO
Spirits:	BEER/WINE	Outdoor Dining:	NO
Parking:	STREET/VALET	Online Menu:	YES

MOZZARELLA FELLA

1668 Main Street
941-366-7600
www.mozzarellafella.com

DOWNTOWN	ITALIAN	COST: $

HOURS: Mon-Sat, 10AM to 5:30PM • CLOSED SUNDAY

INSIDER TIP: One of my favorite downtown lunch spots. Great food. Friendly staff and a super casual experience. Delicious, simple Italians sandwiches. My tip for you, "#10".

WHAT TO EXPECT: Great for lunch • Good lunch meet-up spot
Sandwiches and more • Easy on the wallet

SOME BASICS

Reservations:	NONE	Carry Out:	YES
Credit Cards:	YES	Delivery:	YES
Spirits:	BEER/WINE	Outdoor Dining:	YES
Parking:	STREET	Online Menu:	YES

MUNCHIES 420 CAFÉ

6639 Superior Avenue
941-929-9393
www.munchies420cafe.com

GULF GATE	AMERICAN	COST: $$

HOURS: Daily, 4:20PM to 4:20AM

INSIDER TIP: Yes, this is the *Man vs. Food* place. Late night is their thing. Giant, over the top sandwiches with everything and anything piled on. Grab a Fat Sandy after a night at the pub.

WHAT TO EXPECT: Sandwiches • Super laid back • Late night

SOME BASICS

Reservations:	NONE	Carry Out:	YES
Credit Cards:	YES	Delivery:	YES
Spirits:	FULL BAR	Outdoor Dining:	YES
Parking:	LOT	Online Menu:	YES

MUSE AT THE RINGLING

`NEW`

5401 Bay Shore Road (Ringling Visitors Center)
941-360-7390
www.tableseide.com

NORTH TRAIL	AMERICAN	COST: $$$

HOURS: Lunch, Daily 11AM to 3:30PM
Dinner, Tues-Sat, 3:30PM to 8PM

INSIDER TIP: An excellent choice for an upscale, pre-show dinner. The newest addition to the Tableseide restaurant group. Featuring locally sourced foods, craft beer and wine.

WHAT TO EXPECT: Great wine list • Get you to the show on time
Ringling Museum complex

SOME BASICS

Reservations:	YES	Carry Out:	NO
Credit Cards:	YES	Delivery:	NO
Spirits:	FULL BAR	Outdoor Dining:	YES
Parking:	LOT	Online Menu:	NO

NANCY'S BAR-B-QUE

301 South Pineapple Avenue
941-366-2271
nancysbarbq.com

BURNS COURT	BBQ	COST: $

HOURS: Mon-Thurs, 11AM to 8PM • Fri-Sat, 11AM to 9PM

INSIDER TIP: BBQ. That's what's on the menu. And, great BBQ at that. Brisket, pulled pork, chicken. Walk the serving line and pick your favorites. I recommend the Texas holy trinity!

WHAT TO EXPECT: Great casual dining • Good for families

SOME BASICS

Reservations:	NONE	Carry Out:	YES
Credit Cards:	YES	Delivery:	NO
Spirits:	BEER/WINE	Outdoor Dining:	YES
Parking:	LOT/STREET	Online Menu:	YES

NEW PASS GRILL & BAIT SHOP
1505 Ken Thompson Parkway*
941-388-3050
www.newpassgrill.com

CITY ISLAND	AMERICAN	COST: $

HOURS: Daily, 7AM to 5PM

INSIDER TIP: A Sarasota favorite for locals and visitors alike. A REAL Florida dining experience. "*World Famous - Award Winning Burgers*". But, the view is definitely the main attraction.

WHAT TO EXPECT: Casual dining • Water view • More than burgers
Also a New Pass on St. Armands

SOME BASICS

Reservations:	NONE	Carry Out:	YES
Credit Cards:	YES	Delivery:	NO
Spirits:	BEER/WINE	Outdoor Dining:	YES
Parking:	LOT	Online Menu:	YES

OASIS CAFÉ
3542 South Osprey Avenue
941-957-1214
www.theoasiscafe.net

	AMERICAN	COST: $$

HOURS: Mon-Sat, 7AM to 2PM • Sun, 8AM to 1:30PM

INSIDER TIP: Breakfast and lunch. They have some nice daily specials. Fresh seafood and tasty soups. The blackened basa reuben sandwich is at the top of my personal list.

WHAT TO EXPECT: Breakfast & Lunch • Casual dining

SOME BASICS

Reservations:	NONE	Carry Out:	YES
Credit Cards:	YES	Delivery:	NO
Spirits:	BEER/WINE	Outdoor Dining:	YES
Parking:	LOT	Online Menu:	YES

EAT LIKE A LOCAL
Supporting Locally Owned Restaurants
By Kate Atkin, Sarasota-Manatee Originals

When making dining choices you should really ask yourself: Why is dining at a locally owned restaurant so important?

Every local restaurant is unique and coincides with the culture of the area. Not only is the food unique to the city but so is the atmosphere. National restaurants will be the same no matter where you are in the world, but a local restaurant will offer a one-of-a-kind experience. Each dish is personalized to the area, and the atmosphere gives you the feeling you are in a special place.

While dining at local restaurants, you get to personally know the owners and staff while building a relationship with them. You and the entire community celebrate their success and become emotionally invested. These owners and team members are your neighbors, your friends who care just as much about our community as you do.

When dining at a local restaurant, the money is providing local jobs, sponsoring youth events, and helping the community. In addition, the money boosts the local economy by creating ways for others to spend that money in your city. Studies have shown that for every $100 spent at a local business, $68 will remain in the area compared to $43 when spent at a chain retailer. (Source: Civic Economists)

This means that almost 70% of the money spent at a local restaurant will, in turn, support other local businesses.

I often share this quote as it perfectly sums up the importance of supporting locally owned businesses:

"When you buy from a small business, you are not helping a CEO buy their third vacation home. You are helping a little girl get dance lessons, a little boy get his team jersey, a mom put food on the table, a dad pay a mortgage or a student pay for college" (unknown)

Additionally, locally owned restaurants and businesses are much more involved with community philanthropy than national "big box" restaurants. Ask yourself, when was the last time you saw a community event being supported by "Restaurant XYZ"? Instead, you see the local "Mom & Pop" family-owned restaurants always stepping up to invest in our community.

Another huge advantage when eating at a local independently owned restaurant, you're receiving healthy, fresh food that represents the area's culture.

It's similar to purchasing vegetables and fruits from a local farmers market. You are nutritionally helping yourself and your family and eating healthier than you would in a national chain restaurant. For example, a local seafood restaurant will often purchase seafood from a local fisherman, or a local steak restaurant may purchase their meat from a local farm or ranch.

Also, the more distance there is between the restaurant and the food source, the greater chance there is for less flavor and the potential for food safety issues. Locally grown food shipped to the restaurants are seasonal, full of nutrients, and safer to eat. You will often discover a wider variety that you wouldn't find anywhere else in the world.

Thank you for supporting local businesses and restaurants and remind you to "Eat Like a Local." Happy Dining!

Kate Atkin is the Executive Director of the Sarasota-Manatee Originals. In the theme of supporting local dining establishments, the Sarasota-Manatee Originals is a collaborative group of locally owned restaurants who share a passion for dining excellence and commitment to the community. The Originals boasts 50+ locally owned member restaurants from Anna Maria Island to Venice. www.EatLikeaLocal.com

OFF THE HOOK SEAFOOD COMPANY

6630 Gateway Avenue
941-923-5570
www.offthehookseafoodco.com

GULF GATE	SEAFOOD	COST: $$

HOURS: Tues-Sun, 5PM to 12AM • CLOSED MONDAY

INSIDER TIP: Recently opened in Gulf Gate. Fresh seafood at a good price. Standouts include, fried artichokes. Also, the fresh catch is prepared just about any way that you would like it.

WHAT TO EXPECT: Great for casual seafood • Specialty martinis

SOME BASICS

Reservations:	YES	Carry Out:	YES
Credit Cards:	YES	Delivery:	NO
Spirits:	FULL BAR	Outdoor Dining:	NO
Parking:	LOT	Online Menu:	YES

OH MAMMA MIA!

2324 Gulf Gate Drive
941-706-2821
www.ohmammamiarestaurant.com

GULF GATE	ITALIAN	COST: $$

HOURS: Mon-Thurs, 3:30PM to 9:30PM • Fri-Sat, 2:30PM to 10:30PM

INSIDER TIP: Part circus and part dining. Chef Giuseppe Urbano puts on a live culinary show. The open kitchen showcases his lively style. Penne alla puttanesca tops my list.

WHAT TO EXPECT: Good wine list • Families • OpenTable reservations

SOME BASICS

Reservations:	WEB/PHONE	Carry Out:	YES
Credit Cards:	YES	Delivery:	NO
Spirits:	FULL BAR	Outdoor Dining:	NO
Parking:	LOT	Online Menu:	YES

THE OLD PACKINGHOUSE CAFE

987 South Old Packinghouse Drive
941-371-9358
www.oldpackinghousecafe.com

AMERICAN	COST: $$

HOURS: Mon-Thurs, 11:30AM to 10PM
Fri & Sat, 11:30AM to 11PM

INSIDER TIP: This is a pretty unique Sarasota dining experience. Great food and equally great live music. Love the Cuban sandwich AND the black beans & rice. Fun place!

WHAT TO EXPECT: Live Music • Casual dining • Good for families

SOME BASICS

Reservations:	NONE	Carry Out:	YES
Credit Cards:	YES	Delivery:	NO
Spirits:	FULL BAR	Outdoor Dining:	YES
Parking:	LOT	Online Menu:	YES

THE OLD SALTY DOG

5023 Ocean Boulevard*
941-349-0158
www.theoldsaltydog.com

SIESTA KEY	AMERICAN	COST: $$

HOURS: Lunch & Dinner Daily

INSIDER TIP: Yes. This is the Old Salty Dog featured on *Man vs. Food*. Great island feel whether you're on Siesta, City Island or Venice (2015). Obviously, try a fully loaded Salty Dog. Adam did!

WHAT TO EXPECT: Great for families • Vacation feel • Cold beer
Busy during season • Siesta Village • Friendly bar staff

SOME BASICS

Reservations:	NONE	Carry Out:	YES
Credit Cards:	YES	Delivery:	NO
Spirits:	FULL BAR	Outdoor Dining:	YES
Parking:	STREET	Online Menu:	YES

OPHELIA'S ON THE BAY

9105 Midnight Pass Road
941-349-2212
opheliasonthebay.net

SIESTA KEY	AMERICAN	COST: $$$

HOURS: Dinner Nightly, 5PM to 10PM

INSIDER TIP: Great water views with food to match. The menu boasts American, European and "Floridian". Great seafood choices. The gulf grouper is always a good pick.

WHAT TO EXPECT: Great for a date • Nice water view
Good wine list • OpenTable reservations

SOME BASICS

Reservations:	WEB/PHONE	Carry Out:	YES
Credit Cards:	YES	Delivery:	NO
Spirits:	FULL BAR	Outdoor Dining:	YES
Parking:	VALET	Online Menu:	YES

ORTYGIA

1418 13th Street West
941-741-8646
www.ortygiarestaurant.com

BRADENTON	SICILIAN	COST: $$

HOURS: Lunch, Tue-Sat, 11:30AM to 2:30PM • Dinner, 5PM to 9PM

INSIDER TIP: Sicilian, French and Mediterranean. That's a combo that can please just about everyone. The grilled harissa lamb for an appetizer is certain to get things started right.

WHAT TO EXPECT: Eclectic cuisine • Village of the Arts
OpenTable reservations

SOME BASICS

Reservations:	WEB/PHONE	Carry Out:	YES
Credit Cards:	YES	Delivery:	NO
Spirits:	BEER/WINE	Outdoor Dining:	YES
Parking:	STREET	Online Menu:	YES

OWEN'S FISH CAMP
516 Burns Court
941-951-6936
owensfishcamp.com

BURNS COURT	SEAFOOD	COST: $$

HOURS: Sun-Thurs, 4PM to 9:30PM • Fri-Sat, 4PM to 10:30PM

INSIDER TIP: Cute Burns Court restaurant. Fantastic casual atmosphere. Usually busy, but, they do have a call ahead system. Shrimp & grits are great. But, the low country boil is the standout.

WHAT TO EXPECT: Fun dining experience • Good for families
Decent beer selection • Parking can be a challenge

SOME BASICS
Reservations:	NONE	Carry Out:	YES
Credit Cards:	YES	Delivery:	NO
Spirits:	FULL BAR	Outdoor Dining:	YES
Parking:	STREET/LOT	Online Menu:	YES

PACIFIC RIM
1859 Hillview Street
941-330-8071
pacificrimsarasota.com

SOUTHSIDE VILLAGE	ASIAN	COST: $$

HOURS: Mon-Fri, 11:30AM to 2PM • Mon-Thurs, 5PM to 9:30PM
Fri & Sat, 5PM to 10:30PM • Sun, 5PM to 9PM

INSIDER TIP: Southside's very own sushi mecca. Featuring a beautiful dining room. Inventive sushi and other Asian dishes. Tempura and wok cooking are also available.

WHAT TO EXPECT: Fun dining experience • Sushi
Lots of parking (for Southside Village)

SOME BASICS
Reservations:	4 OR MORE	Carry Out:	YES
Credit Cards:	YES	Delivery:	NO
Spirits:	FULL BAR	Outdoor Dining:	YES
Parking:	LOT/STREET	Online Menu:	YES

PASTRY ART

1512 Main Street
941-955-7545
www.pastryartbakerycafe.com

DOWNTOWN	AMERICAN	COST: $$

HOURS: Mon-Tues, 7AM to 7PM • Thurs, 7AM to 9PM
Wed, Fri & Sat, 7AM to 10PM • Sun, 8AM to 5PM

INSIDER TIP: Fresh baked goods and coffee in the morning, sandwiches in the afternoon. Same afternoon menu as Main Bar Sandwich Shop. Live music including an "open mic" night.

WHAT TO EXPECT: Good downtown meet-up spot • Live music
Cafe • Wi-Fi

SOME BASICS

Reservations:	NONE	Carry Out:	YES
Credit Cards:	YES	Delivery:	NO
Spirits:	BEER/WINE	Outdoor Dining:	YES
Parking:	STREET	Online Menu:	YES

PATRICK'S 1481

1481 Main Street
941-955-1481
www.patricks1481.com

DOWNTOWN	AMERICAN	COST: $$

HOURS: Sun-Wed, 11AM to 10PM • Thurs-Sat, 11AM to 11PM

INSIDER TIP: Burgers! That's what most people think of when they think of Patrick's. And, they do have a great one. The homemade chicken pot pie is fantastic. Good adult bar scene.

WHAT TO EXPECT: Sat. & Sun. Brunch • Sarasota tradition
Good downtown place to meet

SOME BASICS

Reservations:	YES	Carry Out:	YES
Credit Cards:	YES	Delivery:	NO
Spirits:	FULL BAR	Outdoor Dining:	YES
Parking:	STREET	Online Menu:	YES

PATTIGEORGE'S
4120 Gulf of Mexico Drive
941-383-5111
www.pattigeorges.com

LONGBOAT KEY	AMERICAN	COST: $$$

HOURS: Dinner Nightly from 6PM

INSIDER TIP: Longboat fine dining. Chef Tommy Klauber is known for creative and delicious dishes. Beautiful water view. Suggestions, wok about chicken & Thai green curry mussels.

WHAT TO EXPECT: Great for a date • Water view • Great wine list
OpenTable reservations

SOME BASICS
Reservations:	WEB/PHONE	Carry Out:	YES
Credit Cards:	YES	Delivery:	NO
Spirits:	FULL BAR	Outdoor Dining:	NO
Parking:	LOT	Online Menu:	YES

PHILLPPI CREEK OYSTER BAR
5353 South Tamiami Trail
941-925-4444
www.creekseafood.com

SOUTH TRAIL	SEAFOOD	COST: $$

HOURS: Sun-Thurs, 11AM to 10PM • Fri-Sat, 11AM to 10:30PM

INSIDER TIP: Fun for everyone. Casual seafood. Picnic tables and a roll of paper towels casual. Great steamer pots & steamed seafood platters. Try the Maryland spiced shrimp.

WHAT TO EXPECT: Great for families • Water view • Casual dining
Busy during season • Good for kids

SOME BASICS
Reservations:	NO	Carry Out:	YES
Credit Cards:	YES	Delivery:	NO
Spirits:	FULL BAR	Outdoor Dining:	YES
Parking:	LOT	Online Menu:	YES

Craft beer, brew pubs and full on local breweries. Sarasota is not immune from the small batch beer craze. As a matter of fact, we've got some damn good beer craftsmen right here in town. Oh, and along with these local artisans are some great places to down a few unique brews. Here's a list of some of our local favorites. - Cheers!

SARASOTA BREWERIES & BREWPUBS

BIG TOP BREWING
6111 Porter Way
Sarasota, FL 34232
941-371-2939
www.bigtopbrewing.com

CALUSA BREWING
5701 Derek Avenue
Sarasota, FL 34233
941-922-8150
www.calusabrewing.com

DARWIN BREWING COMPANY
803 7th Avenue W
Bradenton, FL 34205
941-747-1970
www.darwinbrewingco.com

JDUB'S BREWING COMPANY
1215 Mango Avenue
Sarasota, FL 34237
941-955-2739
jdubsbrewing.com

MOTORWORKS BREWING
1014 9th Street W
Bradenton, FL 34205
941-567-6218
motorworksbrewing.com

SARASOTA BREWING COMPANY
6607 Gateway Avenue
Sarasota, FL 34231
941-925-2337
www.sarasotabrewing.com

SARASOTA BEER PUBS

MR. BEERY'S
2645 Mall Drive
Sarasota, FL 34231
941-343-2854
www.mrbeeryssrq.com

MANDEVILLE BEER GARDEN
428 N. Lemon Avenue
Sarasota, FL 34236
941-954-8688
www.mandevillebeergarden.com

THE SHAMROCK PUB
2257 Ringling Boulevard
Sarasota, FL 34236
941-952-1730
www.shamrocksarasota.com

WORLD OF BEER
1888 Main Street
Sarasota, FL 34236
941-343-2856
worldofbeer.com

PHO CALI
1578 Main Street
941-955-2683
www.phocalisarasota.com

DOWNTOWN	VIETNAMESE	COST: $

HOURS: Mon-Thurs, 11AM to 9PM • Fri-Sat, 11AM to 9:30PM
CLOSED SUNDAY

INSIDER TIP: Nothing fancy, just great food. First trip to a Vietnamese restaurant? No worries, the staff will help you through the menu. Try the pork & shrimp Vietnamese pancake.

WHAT TO EXPECT: Quick before a show • Casual dining
Easy on the wallet

SOME BASICS
Reservations:	NONE	Carry Out:	YES
Credit Cards:	YES	Delivery:	NO
Spirits:	BEER/WINE	Outdoor Dining:	NO
Parking:	STREET	Online Menu:	YES

PICCOLO ITALIAN MARKET & DELI
6518 Gateway Avenue
941-923-2202
piccolomarket.com

GULF GATE	ITALIAN	COST: $

HOURS: Mon-Sat, 11AM to 6PM • CLOSED SUNDAY

INSIDER TIP: Family owned and it shows. Fantastic Italian style sandwiches. Lots of hard to find Italian market items. Here are some of my favs. Meatball parm & the Tony Soprano sandwich.

WHAT TO EXPECT: Great for a quick lunch • Homemade dishes
Super casual • Easy on the wallet • Catering available

SOME BASICS
Reservations:	NONE	Carry Out:	YES
Credit Cards:	YES	Delivery:	YES
Spirits:	NONE	Outdoor Dining:	NO
Parking:	LOT	Online Menu:	YES

PIER 22

1200 1st Avenue West
941-748-8087
pier22dining.com

BRADENTON	SEAFOOD	COST: $$$

HOURS: Mon-Thurs, 11:30AM to 10PM • Fri-Sat, 11:30AM to 10:30PM
Sun, 11AM to 10PM

INSIDER TIP: Great water view. And, a fantastic menu of seafood dishes. You can also get sushi. They have a nice private event space as well.

WHAT TO EXPECT: Great for a date • Water view • good wine list

SOME BASICS

Reservations:	WEB/PHONE	Carry Out:	YES
Credit Cards:	YES	Delivery:	NO
Spirits:	FULL BAR	Outdoor Dining:	YES
Parking:	LOT	Online Menu:	YES

TOP 25 MENU DOWNLOADS

Lots of you use dineSarasota.com to check out your favorite Sarasota restaurant menu. These were the TOP 25 menus downloads for the past year.

1 - S'macks Burgers
2 - Yoders
3 - Pino's
4 - Lolita Tartine
5 - Libby's Café + Bar
6 - The Bijou Café
7 - Off The Hook Seafood
8 - Turtle's
9 - Andrea's
10 - Polo Grill Bar
11 - Nancy's Bar-B-Que
12 - Eat Here
13 - Rosebud's
14 - Yummy House
15 - Apollonia Grill
16 - Waterfront
17 - The Old Salty Dog
18 - Antoine's
19 - Walt's Fish Market
20 - Anna Maria Oyster Bar
21 - The Table Creekside
22 - Munchies 420 Café
23 - Word of Mouth
24 - Tony's Chicago Beef
25 - Clasico Café

PINO'S

3800 South Tamiami Trail
941-366-1440
www.pinossarasota.com

PARADISE PLAZA	ITALIAN	COST: $$

HOURS: Mon-Thurs, 4PM to 9:30PM • Fri, 4PM to 10PM
Sat, 5PM to 10PM • CLOSED SUNDAY

INSIDER TIP: Pino is back! And, just as good as ever. Pino has been creating exciting Italian fare in Sarasota for a pretty long time. The veal osso bucco is a home run. Get it on special.

WHAT TO EXPECT: Good wine list • Early dining options
Lots of parking • Busy in season

SOME BASICS

Reservations:	YES	Carry Out:	YES
Credit Cards:	YES	Delivery:	NO
Spirits:	BEER/WINE	Outdoor Dining:	YES
Parking:	LOT	Online Menu:	YES

POLO GRILL & BAR

10670 Boardwalk Loop
941-782-0899
www.pologrillandbar.com

LAKEWOOD RANCH	AMERICAN	COST: $$

HOURS: Dinner, Daily from 5:30PM
Lunch, Mon - Sat, 11:30AM to 2:30PM

INSIDER TIP: They were one of the first out in LWR. Always a great meal. A large private event space. Favs include, miso glazed Chilean sea bass & duck cashew spring rolls.

WHAT TO EXPECT: Good wine list • OpenTable reservations
Adult lounge scene • Catering available

SOME BASICS

Reservations:	WEB/PHONE	Carry Out:	YES
Credit Cards:	YES	Delivery:	NO
Spirits:	FULL BAR	Outdoor Dining:	NO
Parking:	LOT/STREET	Online Menu:	YES

POMONA BISTRO & WINE BAR

481 North Orange Avenue
941-706-1677
www.pomonabistroandwine.com

DOWNTOWN	AMERICAN	COST: $$$

HOURS: Dinner, Tues - Sat, 5PM • CLOSED SUNDAY & MONDAY

INSIDER TIP: If you've been around Sarasota long enough to remember Zoria then you get it. Simple, elegant dishes and excellent desserts. Oh, they have a cheese plate. I love that!

WHAT TO EXPECT: Great for a date • Quite ambiance
Good wine list • Fine dining

SOME BASICS

Reservations:	YES	Carry Out:	NO
Credit Cards:	YES	Delivery:	NO
Spirits:	FULL BAR	Outdoor Dining:	NO
Parking:	STREET	Online Menu:	YES

PRIMO! RISTORANTE

8076 North Tamiami Trail
941-359-3690
www.primo-ristorante.com

NORTH TRAIL	ITALIAN	COST: $$

HOURS: Mon-Sat, 4PM to 10PM • Sun, 4PM to 9PM
CLOSED MONDAY

INSIDER TIP: Traditional Italian cuisine. They've been in business 25+ years. Pizza cooked in a wood burning oven. Some standouts, duck balsamico & cod positano.

WHAT TO EXPECT: Great casual Italian • Pizza

SOME BASICS

Reservations:	YES	Carry Out:	YES
Credit Cards:	YES	Delivery:	NO
Spirits:	FULL BAR	Outdoor Dining:	YES
Parking:	LOT	Online Menu:	YES

PUB 32
8383 South Tamiami Trail
941-952-3070
www.irishpub32.com

SOUTH TRAIL	**IRISH**	**COST: $$**

HOURS: Lunch - Daily, 11:30AM to 4PM
Dinner - Daily, 5PM to 9PM

INSIDER TIP: An Irish "Gastropub". Traditional drinks mixed with upgraded cuisine. They throw a great St. Patty's party! Beef & Guinness stew & chicken pot pie.

WHAT TO EXPECT: Great casual dining • Good beer list
Great selection of Irish Whiskey

SOME BASICS
Reservations:	YES	Carry Out:	YES
Credit Cards:	YES	Delivery:	NO
Spirits:	FULL BAR	Outdoor Dining:	YES
Parking:	LOT	Online Menu:	YES

QUEEN OF SHEBA
NEW

34195 North Tamiami Trail
941-359-8000
queenofshebasarasota.com

NORTH TRAIL	**ETHIOPIAN**	**COST: $$**

HOURS: Wed-Thurs, 4PM to 9PM • Fri & Sat, 11AM to 9:30PM
SUNDAY, MONDAY & TUEDAY CLOSED

INSIDER TIP: Who says Sarasota doesn't have a wide spectrum dining scene. How about some classic Ethiopian fare. They feature a combination platter for a cuisine sampling.

WHAT TO EXPECT: World cuisine • Casual dining experience

SOME BASICS
Reservations:	YES	Carry Out:	YES
Credit Cards:	YES	Delivery:	NO
Spirits:	BEER/WINE	Outdoor Dining:	NO
Parking:	LOT	Online Menu:	YES

REV-EL-RY PUB & GRILL
3005 University Parkway
941-355-1218
www.revelrypubandgrill.com

UPARK	AMERICAN	COST: $$

HOURS: Lunch & Dinner, Daily

INSIDER TIP: Great beer, great food. Their list generally sports 30+ craft brews. What do you eat with all of that beer? Bavarian hot soft pretzel sticks? Or, crispy caramel half duck.

WHAT TO EXPECT: Great for a casual night out • Happy hour
Brick oven pizza • Great beer list

SOME BASICS
Reservations:	YES	Carry Out:	YES
Credit Cards:	YES	Delivery:	NO
Spirits:	FULL BAR	Outdoor Dining:	YES
Parking:	LOT	Online Menu:	YES

RIVERHOUSE REEF & GRILL
995 Riverside Drive
941-729-0616
www.riverhousereefandgrill.com

PALMETTO	SEAFOOD	COST: $$

HOURS: Sun-Thurs, 11:30AM to 9PM • Fri & Sat, 11:30AM to 10PM

INSIDER TIP: Fresh Florida seafood and a super gulf view. Lots of seafood choices and enough other options for the non-seafood eaters. Lobster pot pie, seriously! Can't pass on that.

WHAT TO EXPECT: Water front dining • Daily happy hour
Sunday brunch • Regatta Point Marina

SOME BASICS
Reservations:	YES	Carry Out:	YES
Credit Cards:	YES	Delivery:	NO
Spirits:	FULL BAR	Outdoor Dining:	YES
Parking:	LOT	Online Menu:	YES

VONG SQUASH TOAST

Chef Fran Casciato

INGREDIENTS

4 cups, butternut squash, peeled & diced
1 whole, white onion finely chopped
½ cup, cider vinegar
½ cup, maple syrup
1 cup, extra virgin olive oil
1 cup, mascarpone cheese
1 cup, apricot preserves
½ tsp, kosher salt
¼ tsp, white pepper
¼ tsp, red crushed pepper
crackers

METHOD

Pre heat oven to 325.

In a large mixing bowl, toss the squash with half of the olive oil, salt, red crushed pepper and white pepper. Place squash mixture on a sheet pan and roast for 25 minutes or till tender.

Heat the remaining olive oil in a saute pan. Add the onions and cook until tender. DO NOT CARAMELIZE. Add vinegar and reduce till syrupy. Add the syrup and reduce again until thick and jam like.

Remove squash from oven and place in a mixing bowl. Mash with the back of a fork. Fold in the mascarpone, apricot jelly and onion jam. Adjust the seasoning to your liking.

Serve with crackers

Serves 4 as an appetizer

Upscale local cuisine with international flair is the bedrock inspiration for Muse's concept and development. Muse creates menus with an eye for presentation, using fresh and high-quality products and, as its name suggests, treats food as art. The menu offers an array of wines, handcrafted beers and unique cocktails, which complement a revolving menu. Drawing from locally sourced foods, as well as from domestic and foreign fare, Muse introduces intriguing combinations and variations on cuisine which anchor the innovative menu.

ROADSIDE RIB SHACK
2045 Bahia Vista Street
941-330-9597
www.roadsideribshack.com

BBQ	COST: $

HOURS: Mon-Sat, 11AM to 8PM • Sun, 11AM to 7PM

INSIDER TIP: This place is just made for carryouts. There are seats inside, but, to-go is really your best bet. They have "Party Packs" for easy entertaining. Try the smoked chicken!

WHAT TO EXPECT: Good for kids • Quick carryout • Easy on the wallet
Catering available

SOME BASICS
Reservations:	NONE	Carry Out:	YES
Credit Cards:	YES	Delivery:	YES
Spirits:	NONE	Outdoor Dining:	NO
Parking:	LOT	Online Menu:	YES

ROAST RESTAURANT & BAR

1296 First Street
941-953-1971
roastsarasota.com

DOWNTOWN	AMERICAN	COST: $$$

HOURS: Lunch, Mon-Fri, 11:30AM to 2:30PM
Dinner, Daily From 5:30PM

INSIDER TIP: Roast is a fantastic edition to the already crowded downtown dining scene. Large & small plate dishes. "Modern American" cuisine. Yes, a cheese plate option for dessert!

WHAT TO EXPECT: Private dining room • Late afternoon menu
OpenTable reservations • Catering

SOME BASICS

Reservations:	WEB/PHONE	Carry Out:	YES
Credit Cards:	YES	Delivery:	NO
Spirits:	FULL BAR	Outdoor Dining:	YES
Parking:	STREET/VALET	Online Menu:	YES

ROESSLER'S

2033 Vamo Way
941-966-5688
www.roesslersrestaurant.com

SOUTH TRAIL	EUROPEAN	COST: $$$

HOURS: Dinner, Tue-Sat, From 5PM
CLOSED MONDAY

INSIDER TIP: Family owned/operated since 1978. The menu has a NOLA tilt. Lot's of unique dishes to choose from. Try the crispy duckling New Orleans & steak diane.

WHAT TO EXPECT: Good wine list • Private dining room

SOME BASICS

Reservations:	YES	Carry Out:	NO
Credit Cards:	YES	Delivery:	NO
Spirits:	FULL BAR	Outdoor Dining:	YES
Parking:	LOT	Online Menu:	YES

ROSATI'S PIZZA

935 North Beneva Road
941-953-1802
www.myrosatis.com/store-details/Sarasota

SARASOTA COMMONS	PIZZA	COST: $$

HOURS: Mon-Wed, 4PM to 9PM • Thurs, 11AM to 9PM
Fri, 11AM to 10PM • Sat & Sun, Noon to 9PM

INSIDER TIP: Everybody loves Chicago pizza, right? I know we do. If you've got a taste for that right now, Rosati's is a great local option. Chicago Italian beef or combos available too.

WHAT TO EXPECT: Pizza • Eat in, carry out or delivery

SOME BASICS

Reservations:	NO	Carry Out:	YES
Credit Cards:	YES	Delivery:	YES
Spirits:	BEER/WINE	Outdoor Dining:	YES
Parking:	LOT	Online Menu:	YES

ROSEBUD'S STEAKHOUSE & SEAFOOD

2215 South Tamiami Trail
941-918-8771
www.rosebudssarasota.com

SOUTH TRAIL	STEAKHOUSE	COST: $$

HOURS: Tues-Sun, 4PM to 10PM
CLOSED MONDAY

INSIDER TIP: Independently owned steakhouse. So, if you're not looking for the corporate steakhouse experience this is for you. Reasonable pricing. Prime rib (Queen) $18.99? That's great.

WHAT TO EXPECT: Early bird dining • Private dining room
Adult lounge scene

SOME BASICS

Reservations:	YES	Carry Out:	YES
Credit Cards:	YES	Delivery:	NO
Spirits:	FULL BAR	Outdoor Dining:	NO
Parking:	LOT	Online Menu:	YES

ROY'S RESTAURANT

2001 Siesta Drive
941-952-0109
www.roysrestaurant.com

SOUTHGATE	ASIAN	COST: $$$

HOURS: Sun-Thurs, 5:30PM to 9PM • Fri-Sat, 5:30PM to 10PM
Aloha Hour, 4:30PM to 7PM

INSIDER TIP: "Hawaiian Fusion" cuisine. The food is consistently great here. Chef Roy Yamaguchi has put his unique stamp on his menu. I love the, Misoyaki "Butterfish".

WHAT TO EXPECT: Great for a date • Happy hour

SOME BASICS

Reservations:	WEB/PHONE	Carry Out:	YES
Credit Cards:	YES	Delivery:	NO
Spirits:	FULL BAR	Outdoor Dining:	NO
Parking:	LOT/VALET	Online Menu:	YES

THE RUSSIAN HOUSE

6115 South Tamiami Trail
941-735-1151
russianhouse.net

SOUTH TRAIL	RUSSIAN	COST: $$

HOURS: Mon-Sat, 11AM to 9PM
CLOSED SUNDAY

INSIDER TIP: There aren't many choices in town if you have a craving for Russian cuisine. In fact, this may be it. Good food, good prices. Piroshki, vareniki, pelmeni and more!

WHAT TO EXPECT: Casual ethnic cuisine • Easy on the wallet

SOME BASICS

Reservations:	NONE	Carry Out:	YES
Credit Cards:	YES	Delivery:	NO
Spirits:	BEER/WINE	Outdoor Dining:	NO
Parking:	LOT	Online Menu:	YES

RUTH'S CHRIS STEAKHOUSE

6700 South Tamiami Trail
941-942-9442
www.ruthschris.com

SOUTH TRAIL	STEAKHOUSE	COST: $$$

HOURS: Dinner Daily from 4:30PM

INSIDER TIP: I don't need to tell you what this is. It's Ruth's Chris. Big city steakhouse experience. An older crowd here. USDA prime steaks. 500° sizzling plate. Large sides.

WHAT TO EXPECT: Adult crowd • Great service • Good wine list

SOME BASICS

Reservations:	WEB/PHONE	Carry Out:	YES
Credit Cards:	YES	Delivery:	NO
Spirits:	FULL BAR	Outdoor Dining:	NO
Parking:	LOT/VALET	Online Menu:	NO

---

62 BISTROT CREPERIE & FRENCH BISTROT

1962 Hillview Street
941-954-1011
www.bistrotfl.com

SOUTHSIDE VILLAGE	FRENCH	COST: $$

HOURS: Lunch & Dinner, Daily • Breakfast, Sat & Sun From 8:30AM

INSIDER TIP: Classic French bistro food. Crepes are a specialty. Prix fixe menu daily. A large selection of dessert crepes. Busy Southside Village location.

WHAT TO EXPECT: European bistro • Casual dining experience

SOME BASICS

Reservations:	YES	Carry Out:	YES
Credit Cards:	YES	Delivery:	NO
Spirits:	BEER/WINE	Outdoor Dining:	YES
Parking:	LOT/STREET	Online Menu:	NO

SALTWATER CAFE

1071 North Tamiami Trail
941-488-3775
www.saltwatercafe.com

NOKOMIS	SEAFOOD	COST: $$

HOURS: Mon-Sat, 11:30AM to 11PM • Sun, 11AM to 11PM
Sunday Brunch, 11AM to 2:30PM

INSIDER TIP: Chef Rolf has been cooking up dishes in his Nokomis restaurant for years. Local seafood, steaks and more. Lots of daily specials including a "Steam Pot Party".

WHAT TO EXPECT: Good for families • Local seafood • Specials

SOME BASICS

Reservations:	YES	Carry Out:	YES
Credit Cards:	YES	Delivery:	NO
Spirits:	FULL BAR	Outdoor Dining:	NO
Parking:	LOT	Online Menu:	YES

SALUTE! RISTORANTE ENOTECA

23 North Lemon Avenue
941-365-1020
www.salutesarasota.com

DOWNTOWN	ITALIAN	COST: $$

HOURS: Sun-Thurs, 4PM to 10PM • Fri-Sat, 4PM to 11PM

INSIDER TIP: Located right in the heart of downtown Sarasota. Great authentic Italian cuisine. Nice outdoor dining space. They have their own winery in Italy! And, it's good.

WHAT TO EXPECT: Great for a date • Unique wines
OpenTable reservations • Nice outdoor dining

SOME BASICS

Reservations:	WEB/PHONE	Carry Out:	YES
Credit Cards:	YES	Delivery:	NO
Spirits:	FULL BAR	Outdoor Dining:	YES
Parking:	STREET/LOT	Online Menu:	YES

THE SANDBAR

100 Spring Avenue
941-778-0444
sandbar.groupersandwich.com

ANNA MARIA	AMERICAN	COST: $$

HOURS: Lunch & Dinner, Daily • Sunday Brunch, 10AM to 1PM

INSIDER TIP: North end of Anna Maria Island. They feature fresh Florida seafood. Dining on the beach. Feel like you're on vacation even if you're not! Getting married? Great for a wedding!

WHAT TO EXPECT: Great causal beach dining • Island feel
Good for a private beach party

SOME BASICS

Reservations:	NONE	Carry Out:	YES
Credit Cards:	YES	Delivery:	NO
Spirits:	FULL BAR	Outdoor Dining:	YES
Parking:	LOT	Online Menu:	YES

SARASOTA BREWING COMPANY

6607 Gateway Avenue
941-925-2337
www.sarasotabrewing.com

GULF GATE	BREW PUB	COST: $$

HOURS: Mon-Thurs, 11AM to 12AM • Fri-Sat, 11AM to 1AM
Sun, 12PM to 12AM

INSIDER TIP: They were "craft brewing" beer before it was fashionable in Florida. They offer a good selection of styles. Plus, a menu of brew pub fare and Chicago style pizza.

WHAT TO EXPECT: Brew pub • Lots of menu choices

SOME BASICS

Reservations:	NONE	Carry Out:	YES
Credit Cards:	YES	Delivery:	NO
Spirits:	FULL BAR	Outdoor Dining:	NO
Parking:	LOT	Online Menu:	YES

SARDINIA

5770 South Tamiami Trail
941-702-8582
sardiniasrq.com

SOUTH TRAIL	ITALIAN	COST: $$$

HOURS: Mon-Sat, 5PM to 10PM • CLOSED SUNDAY

INSIDER TIP: Traditional Italian cuisine prepared with local ingredients. They have a wood burning oven for bread and braised meats. Veal chop alla brace & spigola al sale.

WHAT TO EXPECT: Good wine list • Intimate atmosphere

SOME BASICS

Reservations:	YES	Carry Out:	YES
Credit Cards:	YES	Delivery:	NO
Spirits:	BEER/WINE	Outdoor Dining:	NO
Parking:	LOT	Online Menu:	YES

SELVA GRILL

1345 Main Street
941-362-4427
www.selvagrill.com

DOWNTOWN	PERUVIAN	COST: $$$

HOURS: Mon-Thurs, 5PM to 11PM • Fri-Sat, 5PM to 1PM

INSIDER TIP: When downtown started it's upscale restaurant renaissance Selva was at the head of the parade. Great ceviche, tapas and Peruvian cuisine. Always lively atmosphere.

WHAT TO EXPECT: Great for a date • Main & Palm • OpenTable

SOME BASICS

Reservations:	WEB/PHONE	Carry Out:	YES
Credit Cards:	YES	Delivery:	NO
Spirits:	FULL BAR	Outdoor Dining:	YES
Parking:	STREET/PALM GARAGE	Online Menu:	YES

SENOR SIESTA

5110 Ocean Boulevard
941-349-0818
www.senorsiesta.com

SIESTA KEY	SPANISH	COST: $$

HOURS: Tues-Sun, 5PM to 10PM • CLOSED MONDAY

INSIDER TIP: The dishes of Spain and Portugal are featured. Not pricey. Great Siesta Village location. Some recommendations include, carne asada plato tipico & arroz con pollo.

WHAT TO EXPECT: Casual Siesta Key • Lots of parking (Siesta Village) Easy on the wallet • Good for kids

SOME BASICS

Reservations:	YES	Carry Out:	YES
Credit Cards:	YES	Delivery:	NO
Spirits:	BEER/WINE	Outdoor Dining:	YES
Parking:	LOT	Online Menu:	YES

SHAKESPEARE'S ENGLISH PUB

3550 South Osprey Avenue
941-364-5938
www.shakespearesenglishpub.com

	BRITISH	COST: $$

HOURS: Mon-Fri, 11:30AM to 11PM • Sat-Sun, 12PM to 11PM

INSIDER TIP: A pretty massive and intimidating beer list. It's BIG. This is a nice, little out of the way pub. Lots of authentic English fare. Bangers & mash, English dustbin lids & sausage rolls.

WHAT TO EXPECT: Great for after work meet-up • Lots of beer Osprey, across from Paradise Plaza

SOME BASICS

Reservations:	NONE	Carry Out:	YES
Credit Cards:	YES	Delivery:	NO
Spirits:	BEER/WINE	Outdoor Dining:	YES
Parking:	LOT	Online Menu:	YES

DRINK, DRINK, DRINK

The Mixologists at Eat Here

WATERMELON MOJITO

MUDDLE
2 or 3 lime wedges (depending on size)
ice cream scoop of watermelon
8-10 mint leaves
¾ oz. simple syrup

Top with ice and 2 ounces of light rum

Shake lightly and fill rest of glass with soda top with
scoop of watermelon and a lime.

BLOODY CAESAR

2 oz. of infused gin
½ oz. of bouillabaisse broth or clam juice
½ oz. of tomato juice
3 turns of the pepper wheel
Dash of salt
3 dashes of Worcestershire sauce
3 dashes of hot sauce (Crystal's)

Shake and serve up. Garnished with an asparagus stalk,
a cherry tomato cut into halves and horseradish sauce.

BEE'S KNEES

2 oz. Bombay Gin
Juice of 1/2 lemon
¾ oz. Honey Lavender Syrup

Shake well and serve up. Top with splash of soda.
Garnish with a twist.

*Sean Murphy and his wife Susan Timmins have owned and
operated the award winning Beach Bistro for thirty years. Sean
is also the founder of the Bistro's more casual cousins, the two
"Eat Here" restaurants on Anna Maria Island and Siesta Key. Eat
Here offers a relaxed, neighborhood friendly atmosphere. The
restaurant is a place for the whole family to enjoy a meal together
every night of the week.*

THE SHAMROCK
2257 Ringling Boulevard
941-952-1730
www.shamrocksarasota.com

DOWNTOWN	IRISH	COST: $

HOURS: Daily, 3PM to 2:30AM

INSIDER TIP: Interesting imported and local beer on tap.
Selection is always changing. In the summer they feature local
chefs cooking outside. Dishes paired with equally great beer.

WHAT TO EXPECT: Fun night out • You can watch soccer
Great St. Patty's Day party

SOME BASICS

Reservations:	NONE	Carry Out:	NO
Credit Cards:	YES	Delivery:	NO
Spirits:	BEER/WINE	Outdoor Dining:	NO
Parking:	STREET	Online Menu:	NO

SHANERS PIZZA

`NEW`

6500 Superior Avenue
941-927-2708
shanerspizza.com

GULF GATE	PIZZA	COST: $$

HOURS: Mon-Fri, 4PM to 10PM • Sat & Sun, 4PM to 12AM

INSIDER TIP: Shaner's is back! Again. This time one of Sarasota's favorite pizza joints appears in Gulf Gate. Good news, same super thin, delicious Shaner's pizza that we love!

WHAT TO EXPECT: Pizza • Eat in or carry out • Open late

SOME BASICS

Reservations:	NONE	Carry Out:	YES
Credit Cards:	YES	Delivery:	NO
Spirits:	BEER/WINE	Outdoor Dining:	YES
Parking:	LOT/STREET	Online Menu:	YES

SHARKEY'S ON THE PIER

1600 Harbor Drive South
941-488-1456
sharkysonthepier.com

VENICE	AMERICAN	COST: $$

HOURS: Sun-Thurs, 11:30AM to 10PM • Fri-Sat, 11:30AM to 12AM

INSIDER TIP: "Smack Dab on the Beach". That's their line. And, it's true. They have a fishing pier too! Casual beach-side dining. Lots of fresh fish on the menu.

WHAT TO EXPECT: Live music • On the beach • Very "Florida"

SOME BASICS

Reservations:	YES	Carry Out:	YES
Credit Cards:	YES	Delivery:	NO
Spirits:	FULL BAR	Outdoor Dining:	YES
Parking:	LOT	Online Menu:	YES

SHORE DINER

465 John Ringling Boulevard
941-296-0301
shorebrand.com

ST. ARMANDS	AMERICAN	COST: $$$

HOURS: Lunch & Dinner Daily

INSIDER TIP: This is one of the Caragiulo owned restaurants. So, you're pretty assured of good food & service. Part of this restaurant is open air. Fun for groups. It's an adult bar scene.

WHAT TO EXPECT: OpenTable reservations • Busy during season
         Good wine list

SOME BASICS

Reservations:	YES	Carry Out:	YES
Credit Cards:	YES	Delivery:	NO
Spirits:	FULL BAR	Outdoor Dining:	YES
Parking:	STREET	Online Menu:	YES

SIESTA KEY OYSTER BAR (SKOB)

5238 Ocean Boulevard
941-346-5443
www.skob.com

SIESTA KEY	AMERICAN	COST: $$

HOURS: Mon-Thurs, 11AM to 12AM • Fri-Sat, 11AM to 2AM
         Sun, 9AM to 12AM

INSIDER TIP: When you hear locals talk about SKOB, this is it! They serve tons of oysters. Great live music and a festive island atmosphere await. Their daily oyster "Happy Hour" is a deal!

WHAT TO EXPECT: Vacation atmosphere • Live music daily
         Siesta Village • Great for families • Busy in season

SOME BASICS

Reservations:	NONE	Carry Out:	YES
Credit Cards:	YES	Delivery:	NO
Spirits:	FULL BAR	Outdoor Dining:	YES
Parking:	LOT/STREET	Online Menu:	YES

S'MACKS BURGERS

2407 Bee Ridge Road
941-922-7673
http://www.geckosgrill.com/smacks-burgers-and-shakes.php

BEE RIDGE	BURGERS	COST: $$

HOURS: Daily, 10AM to 11PM

INSIDER TIP: Locally sourced burger joint. Think Shake Shack and you're on the right track. The burgers and the shakes are good. But, the garlic herb parmesan fries rock! Get them!

WHAT TO EXPECT: Casual burger joint • Shakes
Good for families

SOME BASICS

Reservations:	NONE	Carry Out:	YES
Credit Cards:	YES	Delivery:	NO
Spirits:	NONE	Outdoor Dining:	YES
Parking:	LOT	Online Menu:	YES

SOCIAL EATERY & BAR

1219 First Street
941-444-7072
socialonfirst.com

DOWNTOWN	ITALIAN	COST: $$

HOURS: Sun-Thurs, 5PM to 12AM • Fri-Sat, 5PM to 2AM

INSIDER TIP: They feature a "Meatballeria" section on their menu. No other place in town can say that! Small plate options. Also, wood fired pizza. Obviously, you should try the meatballs!

WHAT TO EXPECT: Great for a date • Nice outdoor dining area
Good wine list • Young adult bar scene

SOME BASICS

Reservations:	WEB/PHONE	Carry Out:	YES
Credit Cards:	YES	Delivery:	NO
Spirits:	FULL BAR	Outdoor Dining:	YES
Parking:	STREET	Online Menu:	YES

SOL MEYER NY DELICATESSEN

1473 Main Street
941-955-3354

DOWNTOWN	DELI	COST: $$

HOURS: Daily, Breakfast, Lunch & Dinner

INSIDER TIP: Real NY deli hits downtown Sarasota. We've been asking for this and now we've got it! Brand new in 2015. Real pastrami sandwiches, knishes and matzo ball soup.

WHAT TO EXPECT: Good for families • Great for carryout
Catering available

SOME BASICS

Reservations:	NONE	Carry Out:	YES
Credit Cards:	YES	Delivery:	NO
Spirits:	NONE	Outdoor Dining:	NO
Parking:	STREET	Online Menu:	NO

SOLORZANO'S BROTHERS PIZZA

3604 Webber Street*
941-926-4276
www.solorzanobros.com

WEBBER/BENEVA	PIZZA	COST: $$

HOURS: Tues-Sat, 11AM to 10PM • Sun, 4PM to 10PM
CLOSED MONDAY

INSIDER TIP: Homemade pies. You can even get it by the slice. A Solorzano Supreme is delicious. But, for me a "Red Tide" (garlic, anchovy & black olive) is too much to resist!

WHAT TO EXPECT: Pizza • They deliver • Lunch specials
"Flour Hour" specials

SOME BASICS

Reservations:	NONE	Carry Out:	YES
Credit Cards:	YES	Delivery:	YES
Spirits:	NONE	Outdoor Dining:	NO
Parking:	LOT	Online Menu:	YES

SOLORZANO'S RISTORANTE

6516 Superior Avenue
941-906-9444

GULF GATE	ITALIAN	COST: $$

HOURS: Tues-Sat, 5PM to 10PM • CLOSED SUNDAY & MONDAY

INSIDER TIP: If you're from Hoboken NJ then this is your go-to place. If you're not, you will still enjoy a great homemade Italian meal. Finish your meal with a slice of cheesecake!

WHAT TO EXPECT: Casual Italian • Good wine list • Quite atmosphere

SOME BASICS

Reservations:	YES	Carry Out:	YES
Credit Cards:	YES	Delivery:	NO
Spirits:	BEER/WINE	Outdoor Dining:	YES
Parking:	LOT/STREET	Online Menu:	NO

SQUARE 1 BURGERS

6240 South Tamiami Trail*
941-870-8111
www.square1burgers.com

SOUTH TRAIL	BURGERS	COST: $$

HOURS: Sun-Thurs, 11AM to 11PM • Fri-Sat, 11AM to 12AM

INSIDER TIP: Burgers. The name says it. This is a mini-chain. But, it still maintains an independent feel. Burgers from Angus beef, turkey, chicken, buffalo and more. Rise & shine burger!

WHAT TO EXPECT: Good for families • Burgers, burgers, burgers
Busy in season • Changed location 2015

SOME BASICS

Reservations:	NONE	Carry Out:	YES
Credit Cards:	YES	Delivery:	NO
Spirits:	FULL BAR	Outdoor Dining:	NO
Parking:	LOT	Online Menu:	YES

THE STARLITE ROOM

1001 Cocoanut Avenue
941-702-5613
www.starlitesrq.com

DOWNTOWN	AMERICAN	COST: $$

HOURS: Daily from 4PM

INSIDER TIP: This is the old Broadway Bar. New owners, new feel. Lots of good small and large plate options. A convenient place to eat before a Van Wezel show.

WHAT TO EXPECT: Great before/after show • Small plate
Good cocktail list

SOME BASICS

Reservations:	YES	Carry Out:	YES
Credit Cards:	YES	Delivery:	NO
Spirits:	FULL BAR	Outdoor Dining:	NO
Parking:	STREET	Online Menu:	YES

STATE STREET EATING HOUSE

1533 State Street
941-951-1533
statestreetsrq.com

DOWNTOWN	AMERICAN	COST: $$

HOURS: Tues-Sat, 11:30AM to 11:30PM
CLOSED SUNDAY & MONDAY

INSIDER TIP: Love the feel of this place. Casual, but, big city at the same time. You could easily imagine this place in Seattle WA. Baked lobster mac & cheese". You could eat the whole menu!

WHAT TO EXPECT: Great for a date • Comfort food • Good wine list

SOME BASICS

Reservations:	5 OR MORE	Carry Out:	YES
Credit Cards:	YES	Delivery:	NO
Spirits:	FULL BAR	Outdoor Dining:	NO
Parking:	LOT	Online Menu:	YES

STATION 400

400 Lemon Avenue*
941-906-1400
www.station400.com

ROSEMARY	AMERICAN	COST: $$

HOURS: Daily, 8AM to 3PM

INSIDER TIP: Chef driven, creative breakfast and lunch dishes. No reservations, it's usually busy. Here are some ideas. Truffle eggs benedict & lemon poached shrimp salad. Great place.

WHAT TO EXPECT: Great for lunch meet-up • Lots of pancakes
Soups, salads & sandwiches

SOME BASICS

Reservations:	NONE	Carry Out:	YES
Credit Cards:	YES	Delivery:	NO
Spirits:	BEER/WINE	Outdoor Dining:	YES
Parking:	LOT	Online Menu:	YES

STOTTLEMEYER'S SMOKEHOUSE

19 East Road
941-312-5969
www.stottlemyerssmokehouse.com

	BBQ	COST: $$

HOURS: Tues-Thurs, 11:30AM to 8:30PM • Fri-Sat, 11AM to 10PM
Sun, 11:30PM to 8:30PM • CLOSED MONDAY

INSIDER TIP: "Classic BBQ Meets Old Florida", that's their motto. And, for a change it's pretty right on. Great BBQ and an old Florida feel to the place. Fantastic fried chicken too.

WHAT TO EXPECT: Good for families • Easy on the wallet
Live music • Casual Florida dining experience

SOME BASICS

Reservations:	YES	Carry Out:	YES
Credit Cards:	YES	Delivery:	NO
Spirits:	FULL BAR	Outdoor Dining:	YES
Parking:	LOT	Online Menu:	YES

SUN GARDEN CAFÉ
210 Avenida Madera
941-346-7170
sungardencafe.net

| SIESTA KEY | AMERICAN | COST: $$ |

HOURS: Daily, 7:30AM to 2:30PM

INSIDER TIP: Siesta Village. Casual breakfast and lunch spot. Comfortable outdoor seating area. Creative dishes highlight the menu. Love the BLT w/avocado & the curried chicken soup.

WHAT TO EXPECT: Casual island lunch • Nice outdoor seating
Sandwich/soup/salad combos

SOME BASICS

Reservations:	NONE	Carry Out:	YES
Credit Cards:	YES	Delivery:	NO
Spirits:	BEER/WINE	Outdoor Dining:	YES
Parking:	STREET	Online Menu:	YES

SURF SHACK COASTAL KITCHEN   `NEW`
326 John Ringling Boulevard
941-960-1122
www.surfshackkitchen.com

| ST. ARMANDS | AMERICAN | COST: $$ |

HOURS: Sun-Thurs, 11:30AM to 10PM • Fri & Sat, 11:30AM to 12AM

INSIDER TIP: Gourmet tacos. Yes, that's a thing in Sarasota now. Relaxed and casual. Just the way a taco shop should be. Great guacamole too. Oh, don't forget upstairs, The Terrace.

WHAT TO EXPECT: Rooftop dining • Busy in season • Open late

SOME BASICS

Reservations:	YES	Carry Out:	YES
Credit Cards:	YES	Delivery:	NO
Spirits:	FULL BAR	Outdoor Dining:	YES
Parking:	LOT/STREET	Online Menu:	YES

dineSarasota Essentials

GET HAPPY
By Nita Ettinger, Must Do Magazine

Here is a carefully selected list of my favorite Happy Hour spots. I hope they help take the guesswork out of where to find a great drink or bite to eat!

Best Craft Beer Bar/ Best Beer Menu
Mr. Beery's (2645 Mall Drive) - Mondays $3 pint night – all day!

World of Beer (1888 Main Street) - Boasts 550+ beers from around the world. Also located near UTC Mall & Bradenton.

Mandeville Beer Garden (428 N. Lemon Avenue) – Choose from 30 taps, 150 bottles, specials include $1 off drafts from 4 to 7 p.m.

Best Cocktail Bar/ Cocktail Menu
Pangea Lounge (1568 Main Street) – Creative drinks from an award-winning bartender. Late night Happy Hour is a big hit.

Social Eatery & Bar (1219 1st Street) - While the drinks aren't offered at a discount price the variety of specialty craft cocktails and the fantastic outdoor patio make this a standout spot.

Best View
Blue Sunshine Patio Bar & Grill at Marina Jack (2 Marina Plaza) Offers a marina view of Sarasota Bay. Furry family members welcome at this dog-friendly bar with nightly live music. Drink specials and Happy Hour menu Monday through Friday from 4 to 6 p.m.

Fins at Sharky's on the Pier (1600 Harbor Drive S) – Venice waterfront location on the Gulf of Mexico. Fins offers $5 - $6 handcrafted cocktails and wine, plus $6 sushi rolls, flatbreads and more from 4 to 6 p.m.

Phillippi Creek Restaurant & Oyster Bar (5353 S. Tamiami Trail) - Phillippi Creek waterfront location. Drink specials from 3 to 5:30 p.m. includes $3 Sailor Jerry Spiced Rum, house margaritas, $2.50 draft pints, $4 house wine, $5 martinis, $4.50 well drinks. Order from the bar and enjoy your drinks in the outdoor tiki hut.

Best Wine Bar / Best Wine List, Wine by the Glass

Fleming's Prime Steakhouse' Wine Bar (2001 Siesta Drive) Features 5 cocktails, 5 wines by the glass, 5 appetizers and other specials for $6 from 5 until 7. Late night offerings 8 for $9 until 10 p.m.

Michael's on East (1212 S. East Street) – Enjoy Michael's Private Label Wines, Draft Beers & Well Cocktails in the Lounge from 5 to 7 p.m. Check their Facebook page on Monday for the "secret word" of the day to receive a free appetizer. Special extended Monday Happy Hour supports local charities from July through September.

Go for Happy Hour, Stay for the Music

SKOB (5238 Ocean Boulevard) – Always hoppin' in the heart of Siesta Key Village. Grab some half-price oysters or Louisiana Crawfish along with drink specials from 3 to 6 p.m. Late night Happy Hour drink specials from 10 to close.

Blue Rooster (1525 4th Street) – Enjoy $4 wells, $1 off all beer, $5 martinis, $4 house wines, $3, $5 & $7 appetizers from 5 to 7 p.m. Then stick around for a variety of local and national music acts.

Best Bar To Catch The Game

Gecko's (4870 S. Tamiami Trail) – Multiple locations & TVs to help you root for your team. Two-for-one cocktails, margaritas, martinis, frozen drinks and house wines all day every day.

Nita Ettinger is the co-publisher for Siesta Publications and Editor for Must Do Visitor Guides. Must Do Visitor Guides provides Southwest Florida visitor information through printed publications and the website MustDo.com. Must Do visitor guides are published bi-annually and are available at no cost in Sarasota, Lee and Collier County chambers of commerce, visitor information centers, select Southwest Florida hotels and wherever free publications are found.

THE TABLE CREEKSIDE
5365 South Tamiami Trail
941-921-9465
tablesrq.com

SOUTH TRAIL	AMERICAN	COST: $$$

HOURS: Sun-Thurs, 4PM to 10PM • Fri-Sat, 4PM to 10:30PM

INSIDER TIP: Waterside upscale dining. Daily chef selections are featured as is a dynamite "Happy Hour". Some favs include, lemon roasted Chilean sea bass & the poached pear salad.

WHAT TO EXPECT: Great for a date • Water view • Good wine list
Happy hour • Daily specials

SOME BASICS
Reservations:	YES	Carry Out:	YES
Credit Cards:	YES	Delivery:	NO
Spirits:	FULL BAR	Outdoor Dining:	YES
Parking:	LOT	Online Menu:	YES

TANDOOR
8453 Cooper Creek Boulevard
941-926-3070
tandoorsarasota.net

UPARK	INDIAN	COST: $$

HOURS: Lunch Daily, 11:30AM to 2:30PM
Dinner, Sun-Thurs, 5PM to 9:30PM • Fri & Sat, 5PM to 10PM

INSIDER TIP: Consistently good Indian cuisine. A wide variety of choices on their menu. If you're an Indian cuisine beginner, they will help you through that first experience.

WHAT TO EXPECT: Great for group • Tandoor cooking

SOME BASICS
Reservations:	YES	Carry Out:	YES
Credit Cards:	YES	Delivery:	NO
Spirits:	BEER/WINE	Outdoor Dining:	NO
Parking:	LOT	Online Menu:	YES

TASTE OF ASIA
4413 South Tamiami Trail
941-923-2742
www.tasteofasiasrq.com

SOUTH TRAIL	LAOTIAN/THAI	COST: $$

HOURS: Lunch, Wed-Sat, 11:30AM to 2:30PM
Dinner, Nightly • CLOSED MONDAY

INSIDER TIP: Family owned and operated. Fantastic
Laotian,Vietnamese & Thai cuisine. The real deal. The Lum-plings
and pho dishes are excellent. Cauliflower fried rice is great!

WHAT TO EXPECT: Fun night out • Good for families
Busy in season • Beginners welcome • Cooking classes

SOME BASICS
Reservations:	YES	Carry Out:	YES
Credit Cards:	YES	Delivery:	NO
Spirits:	FULL BAR	Outdoor Dining:	YES
Parking:	LOT	Online Menu:	YES

TASTY HOME COOKIN'
3854 South Tuttle Avenue
941-921-4969
tastyhomecookinsarasota.com

TUTTLE BEE PLAZA	AMERICAN	COST: $

HOURS: Mon-Fri, 7AM to 8PM • Sat, 7AM to 3PM
Sun, 8AM to 3PM

INSIDER TIP: This place is a one of a kind. In business for 22+
years. The "Tasty Burgers" are a like a White Castle slider. They
come 3 to an order. Lots of comfort food on the menu.

WHAT TO EXPECT: Great for families • Easy on the wallet
Comfort food • Casual dining • Good for kids

SOME BASICS
Reservations:	NONE	Carry Out:	YES
Credit Cards:	YES	Delivery:	NO
Spirits:	BEER/WINE	Outdoor Dining:	NO
Parking:	LOT	Online Menu:	YES

THAILAND RESTAURANT

2238 Gulf Gate Drive
941-927-8424
www.thailandsarasota.com

GULF GATE	ASIAN	COST: $$

HOURS: Lunch: Mon-Sat, 11:30AM to 2:30PM
Dinner: Mon-Thurs, 5PM to 9:30PM • Fri & Sat, 5PM to 10PM
Sun, 5PM to 9PM

INSIDER TIP: Simple & great! Sushi + Thai cuisine. Place where locals eat. Bruce swears by the Vietnamese pork fried rice.

WHAT TO EXPECT: Big menu • Noodles, curry and much more

SOME BASICS

Reservations:	YES	Carry Out:	YES
Credit Cards:	YES	Delivery:	NO
Spirits:	FULL BAR	Outdoor Dining:	YES
Parking:	STREET	Online Menu:	YES

TOASTED MANGO CAFE

430 North Tamiami Trail*
941-388-7728
www.toastedmangocafe.com

NORTH TRAIL	AMERICAN	COST: $$

HOURS: Daily, 7AM to 3PM

INSIDER TIP: This breakfast & lunch spot sets a pretty high bar for everyone else. Fresh, healthy menu items and excellent service. Just opened a second location on Siesta Key.

WHAT TO EXPECT: Good for families • Casual dining • Great service
Lots of menu choices

SOME BASICS

Reservations:	NONE	Carry Out:	YES
Credit Cards:	YES	Delivery:	NO
Spirits:	FULL BAR	Outdoor Dining:	NO
Parking:	LOT	Online Menu:	YES

TOMMY BAHAMA CAFÉ

300 John Ringling Boulevard
941-388-2888
www.tommybahama.com

ST. ARMANDS	AMERICAN	COST: $$

HOURS: Lunch & Dinner Daily, 11AM

INSIDER TIP: How about a little island shopping followed by a little island lunching? Tommy Bahama's is terrific for both. It's a first-class menu of casual cuisine.

WHAT TO EXPECT: Great for relaxing lunch • Island time happy hour
St. Armands Circle

SOME BASICS

Reservations:	YES	Carry Out:	YES
Credit Cards:	YES	Delivery:	NO
Spirits:	FULL BAR	Outdoor Dining:	YES
Parking:	STREET	Online Menu:	YES

TONY'S CHICAGO BEEF

6569 Superior Avenue
941-922-7979
www.tonyschicagobeef.com

GULF GATE	AMERICAN	COST: $

HOURS: Mon-Thurs, 11AM to 9PM • Fri-Sat, 11AM to 10PM
CLOSED SUNDAY

INSIDER TIP: Looking for REAL Chicago style food? This is it! Fantastic beef sandwiches and double cooked French fries. Chicago dogs, burgers and pizza puffs. Windy city all the way!

WHAT TO EXPECT: Great for lunch • Easy on the wallet
Chicago style food • Counter and table seating

SOME BASICS

Reservations:	NONE	Carry Out:	YES
Credit Cards:	YES	Delivery:	YES
Spirits:	BEER/WINE	Outdoor Dining:	YES
Parking:	LOT/STREET	Online Menu:	YES

LOCAL FARMERS MARKET INFORMATION

SARASOTA FARMER'S MARKET
Lemon Avenue
Downtown Sarasota
Saturday's (Year Round)
7AM to 1PM
Rain or Shine
70 Vendors
www.sarasotafarmersmarket.org

THE MARKET AT FIVE POINTS
Sarasota Farmer's Market
Five Points Park (1st Street & N. Pineapple Avenue)
Wednesday's (Nov. thru April)
10AM to 2PM

CENTRAL SARASOTA FARMER'S MARKET
Florida House (4454 S. Beneva Rd.)
Fall, Winter, Spring
8AM to 1PM
Rain or Shine
centralsarasotafarmersmarket.com

SIESTA KEY FARMER'S MARKET
Davidson's Plaza (Ocean Boulevard)
Sunday's (Year Round)
9AM to 2PM
Rain or Shine
www.siestafarmersmarket.com

PHILLIPPI FARMHOUSE MARKET
Phillippi Estates Park (5500 South Tamiami Trail)
Wednesday's (Oct. Thru April)
9AM to 2PM
35+ Vendors
farmhousemarket.org

VENICE FARMER'S MARKET
Downtown Venice (Tampa Ave. & Nokomis Ave.)
Saturday's (Year Round)
8AM to 12PM
thevenicefarmersmarket.com

WHAT'S IN SEASON?

Now you have a pretty good idea where to buy the freshest locally grown produce. But, what's the best time of year to enjoy Florida's fruits and vegetables? When are they at their peak of freshness? Here's a little help.

WINTER > Avocado • Bell Pepper • Egg Plant • Grapefruit
Strawberries • Squash • Tomatoes
SPRING > Cantaloupe • Guava • Lettuce • Mushrooms
Oranges • Papaya • Radish • Swiss Chard
SUMMER > Avocado • Carambota • Guava • Mango
Peanuts • Sweet Corn • Watermelon • Snow Peas
FALL > Cucumber • Grapefruit • Mushrooms • Oranges
Snap Beans • Tangerines • Tomatoes • Peppers

We have super fresh seafood here in Sarasota. You can usually find a plentiful supply of grouper, red snapper, pompano and mahi at our farmers markets. Of course, you can always find fresh gulf shrimp in a variety of sizes.

The most anticipated seafood season runs from October 15th through May 15th. That's stone crab season! You're best off to grab these beauties towards the beginning of season when they're the most plentiful.

TURTLES ON LITTLE SARASOTA BAY
8875 Midnight Pass Road
941-346-2207
www.turtlesrestaurant.com

SIESTA KEY	AMERICAN	COST: $$

HOURS: Lunch & Dinner, Daily from 11:30AM
Sunday Brunch, 10AM to 3PM • Early Bird 3PM to 6PM

INSIDER TIP: Sure, it's older. But, it has a fantastic water view and the food is good. An older crowd for sure. Some ideas, Georges Bank sea scallops and Turtles crab cakes.

WHAT TO EXPECT: Right on the water • Old, style Florida dining
Sunday brunch • Happy hour specials

SOME BASICS

Reservations:	YES	Carry Out:	YES
Credit Cards:	YES	Delivery:	NO
Spirits:	FULL BAR	Outdoor Dining:	YES
Parking:	LOT	Online Menu:	YES

TWO SENORITA'S RESTAURANT
1355 Main Street
941-366-1618
www.twosenoritas.com

DOWNTOWN	MEXICAN	COST: $$

HOURS: Mon-Thurs, 11:30AM to 10:30PM • Fri-Sat, 11:30AM to 12AM
Sun, 11:30AM to 10PM

INSIDER TIP: Main Street Mexican. This part of Main is now super busy. Sit street-side and watch all the action. Perfect margaritas. Try, shrimp chipotle & ancho encrusted salmon.

WHAT TO EXPECT: Great for a date • Lots to choose from
Good for families

SOME BASICS

Reservations:	YES	Carry Out:	YES
Credit Cards:	YES	Delivery:	NO
Spirits:	FULL BAR	Outdoor Dining:	YES
Parking:	STREET	Online Menu:	YES

VEG
2164 Gulf Gate Drive
941-312-6424
www.vegsrq.com

GULF GATE	VEGETARIAN	COST: $$

HOURS: Lunch Mon-Sat, 11AM to 2:30PM
Dinner, Mon-Sat, from 5PM • CLOSED SUNDAY

INSIDER TIP: Lots of vegetarian and vegan dishes. But, also some seafood. One of Sarasota's best vegetarian restaurants. They serve a pretty respectable matzo ball soup!

WHAT TO EXPECT: Vegan/Veg • Daily specials

SOME BASICS
Reservations:	YES	Carry Out:	YES
Credit Cards:	YES	Delivery:	NO
Spirits:	BEER/WINE	Outdoor Dining:	NO
Parking:	LOT/STREET	Online Menu:	YES

VENEZIA
373 St. Armands Circle
941-388-1400
www.venezia-1966.com

ST ARMANDS	ITALIAN	COST: $$

HOURS: Daily, 11AM to 10PM

INSIDER TIP: Artisan pizza. Also, a full menu of traditional Italian dishes. But, go for the pizza. Sit outside and people watch on St. Armands circle. 15+ specialty pizza pies on the menu.

WHAT TO EXPECT: Great for a date • Pizza
Vibrant atmosphere • Busy during season/weekends

SOME BASICS
Reservations:	YES	Carry Out:	YES
Credit Cards:	YES	Delivery:	NO
Spirits:	FULL BAR	Outdoor Dining:	YES
Parking:	STREET	Online Menu:	YES

VILLAGE CAFÉ

5133 Ocean Boulevard
941-349-2822
www.villagecafeonsiesta.com

SIESTA KEY	AMERICAN	COST: $$

HOURS: Daily, 7AM to 2:30PM

INSIDER TIP: Siesta Key's "neighborhood" restaurant. A local gathering place. Great breakfasts & lunches. Lots of locals make this a daily stop. Daily specials and soups. Super service!

WHAT TO EXPECT: Great for breakfast • Specials daily
Casual dining • Heart of Siesta Village • Good for kids

SOME BASICS

Reservations:	NONE	Carry Out:	YES
Credit Cards:	YES	Delivery:	NO
Spirits:	BEER/WINE	Outdoor Dining:	YES
Parking:	STREET	Online Menu:	YES

WALT'S FISH MARKET

4144 South Tamiami Trail
941-921-4605
www.waltsfishmarketrestaurant.com

SOUTH TRAIL	SEAFOOD	COST: $$

HOURS: Daily, 11AM to 10PM • Market, 9AM to 9PM
Chickee Bar, 11AM to 11PM

INSIDER TIP: Fresh local seafood. It doesn't get any fresher than this! The market has a HUGE selection. Don't forget the smoked mullet spread. That's a Walt's trademark!

WHAT TO EXPECT: Restaurant & market • Live music • Casual dining
Busy in season

SOME BASICS

Reservations:	NONE	Carry Out:	YES
Credit Cards:	YES	Delivery:	NO
Spirits:	FULL BAR	Outdoor Dining:	YES
Parking:	LOT	Online Menu:	YES

WATERFRONT
7660 South Tamiami Trail
941-921-1916
waterfrontoo.com

SOUTH TRAIL	AMERICAN	COST: $$$

HOURS: Dinner Daily, 4PM to 10PM

INSIDER TIP: Serving "The Finest Steaks & Seafood" since 1986. Nice outdoor dining space. It's an old Florida experience. Consistently good food & service. Everybody loves surf & turf!

WHAT TO EXPECT: Great casual steaks & seafood • Water view
An early dining crowd • Daily specials

SOME BASICS

Reservations:	YES	Carry Out:	YES
Credit Cards:	YES	Delivery:	NO
Spirits:	FUL BAR	Outdoor Dining:	YES
Parking:	LOT	Online Menu:	YES

WORD OF MOUTH
6604 Gateway Avenue*
941-925-2400
www.originalwordofmouth.com

GULF GATE	AMERICAN	COST: $$

HOURS: Daily, 8AM to 2PM

INSIDER TIP: Several locations. Gulf Gate is the original. Super casual breakfast & lunch. Good variety of daily specials. A big list of specialty sandwiches. Try a Heather's delight.

WHAT TO EXPECT: Daily specials • Casual dining • Good for families

SOME BASICS

Reservations:	NONE	Carry Out:	YES
Credit Cards:	YES	Delivery:	NO
Spirits:	BEER/WINE	Outdoor Dining:	NO
Parking:	LOT/STREET	Online Menu:	YES

YO SUSHI!

140 University Town Center Drive
941-313-7091
www.yosushi.com

UTC	SUSHI	COST: $$

HOURS: Daily, 11AM to 9PM

INSIDER TIP: Can conveyor belt sushi catch on in Sarasota. We will find out soon enough. Yo Sushi offers one of the areas most unique dining experiences. You have to really pay attention.

WHAT TO EXPECT: Sushi • UTC Mall • Fun for a group

SOME BASICS

Reservations:	NO	Carry Out:	YES
Credit Cards:	YES	Delivery:	NO
Spirits:	BEER/WINE	Outdoor Dining:	NO
Parking:	LOT	Online Menu:	NO

YODER'S RESTAURANT

3434 Bahia Vista
941-955-7771
www.yodersrestaurant.com

PINECRAFT	AMISH	COST: $

HOURS: Mon-Thurs, 6AM to 8PM • Fri-Sat, 6AM to 9PM
CLOSED SUNDAY

INSIDER TIP: Home cooked comfort food at it's best! As seen on *Man vs. Food*. Delicious pies! Everything homemade and it tastes that way. I highly recommend the turkey manhattan!

WHAT TO EXPECT: Great for a families • Easy on the wallet
Busy in season • Fantastic service • Pie

SOME BASICS

Reservations:	NONE	Carry Out:	YES
Credit Cards:	YES	Delivery:	NO
Spirits:	NONE	Outdoor Dining:	NO
Parking:	LOT	Online Menu:	YES

YUME SUSHI

1532 Main Street
941-363-0604
www.yumerestaurant.com

DOWNTOWN	SUSHI	COST: $$

HOURS: Lunch, Mon-Sat, 11:30AM to 2:30PM
Dinner daily from 5PM

INSIDER TIP: One of the top sushi places in town. Creative sushi offerings expertly prepared. Now in a larger downtown, Main Street location. Reservations for parties of 6+.

WHAT TO EXPECT: Great for a date • Fun dining experience

SOME BASICS

Reservations:	6 R MORE	Carry Out:	YES
Credit Cards:	YES	Delivery:	NO
Spirits:	BEER/WINE	Outdoor Dining:	NO
Parking:	STREET	Online Menu:	NO

YUMMY HOUSE

3232 North Tamiami Trail
941-351-1688
yummyhouseflorida.com

NORTH TRAIL	ASIAN	COST: $$

HOURS: Lunch, Daily, 11AM to 2:30PM • Dim Sum, 11AM to 2:30PM
Dinner, Daily, 5PM to 9:30PM

INSIDER TIP: When this place first opened you couldn't get in. Now at least you have a chance. THE Chinese restaurant in town. Dine in or carry out. Try one of the "salt & pepper" dishes.

WHAT TO EXPECT: Busy in season • Lively atmosphere

SOME BASICS

Reservations:	YES	Carry Out:	YES
Credit Cards:	YES	Delivery:	NO
Spirits:	FULL BAR	Outdoor Dining:	NO
Parking:	LOT	Online Menu:	YES

Restaurant Name	Address	Phone #
Adriatico	6606 Superior Ave	922-3080
Amore By Andrea	555 Bay Isles Pkwy	383-1111
Andrea's	2085 Siesta Dr	951-9200
Anna Maria Oyster Bar	6906 14th St W	758-7880
Anna Maria Oyster Bar	6696 Cortez Rd	792-0077
Anna Maria Oyster Bar	1525 51st Ave E	721-7773
Anna's Deli	6535 Midnight Pass	349-4888
Anna's Deli	8207 Tourist Ctr Dr	893-5908
Antoine's Restaurant	5020 Fruitville Rd	377-2020
Apollonia Grill	8235 Cooper Creek	359-4816
Baker & Wife	2157 Siesta Dr	960-1765
Barnacle Bills Seafood	1526 Main St	365-6800
Barnacle Bills Seafood	5050 N. Tamiami Trl	355-7700
Beach Bistro	6600 Gulf Dr N	778-6444
BeachHouse Restaurant	200 Gulf Dr N	779-2222
Big Water Fish Market	6641 Midhight Pass	554-8101
Bijou Cafe	1287 First St	366-8111
Blase Cafe	5263 Ocean Blvd	349-9822
Blu Kouzina	25 N Blvd of Pres.	388-2619
Blu Que Island Grill	149 Avenida Messina	346-0738
Blue Rooster	1524 4th St	388-7539
Boatyard Waterfront Grl	1500 Stickney Pt Rd	921-6200
Bonjour French Cafe	5214 Ocean Blvd	346-0600
The Breakfast House	1817 Fruitville Rd.	366-6860
The Broken Egg	4031 Clark Rd	922-2868
Burns Court Cafe	401 S Pineapple Ave	312-6633
Cafe Don Giovanni	5610 Gulf of Mexico Dr	383-0013
Cafe Epicure	1298 Main St	366-5648

Restaurant Name	Address	Phone #
Cafe Gabbiano	5104 Ocean Blvd	349-1423
Cafe L'Europe	431 St Armands Cir	388-4415
Cafe Venice	116 W. Venice Ave.	484-1855
Capt. Brian's Seafood	8421 N Tamiami Trl	351-4491
Capt. Curt's Oyster Bar	1200 Old Stickney Pt	349-3885
Caragiulos	69 S Palm Ave	951-0866
Carmel Cafe	8433 Cooper Crk Blvd	893-5955
Casey Key Fish House	801 Blackburn Pt Rd	966-1901
C'est La Vie!	1553 Main St	906-9575
Cha Cha Coconuts	417 St Armands Cir	388-3300
Chutney's, Etc.	1944 Hillview Dr	954-4444
Clasico Cafe + Bar	1341 Main St	957-0700
Clayton's Siesta Grille	1256 Old Stickney Pt	349-2800
Coffee Carrousel	1644 Main St	365-2826
The Columbia	411 St Armands Cir	388-3987
Corkscrew Deli	4982 S Tamiami Trl	925-3955
Cosimo's Trattoria	3501 Palmer Crossing	922-7999
The Cottage	153 Avenida Messina	312-9300
Crab & Fin	420 St. Armands Cir	388-3964
Currents	1000 Blvd of the Arts	953-1234
Curry Station	1303 N Washington	312-6264
Curry Station	3550 Clark Road	924-7222
The Crow's Nest	1968 Tarpon Ctr Dr	484-9551
Daiquiri Deck Raw Bar	5250 Ocean Blvd	349-8697
Daiquiri Deck Raw Bar	325 John Ringling Blvd	388-3325
Daiquiri Deck Raw Bar	300 W Venice Ave	488-0649
DaRuMa Japanese	5459 Fruitville Rd	342-6600

Restaurant Name	Address	Phone #
Demetrio's Restaurant	4410 S Tamiami Trl	922-1585
Der Dutchman	3713 Bahia Vista	955-8007
Derek's Rustic Coastal	5516 Manatee Ave	794-1100
Dolce Italia	6606 Superior Ave	921-7007
Drunken Poet Cafe	1572 Main St	955-8404
Dry Dock Waterfront	412 Gulf of Mexico Dr	383-0102
Dutch Valley Restaurant	6731 S Tamiami Trl	924-1770
Duval's New World Cafe	1435 Main St	312-4001
Eat Here	240 Avenida Madera	346-7800
El Greco Cafe	1592 Main St	365-2234
El Toro Bravo	2720 Stickney Pt	924-0006
Euphemia Haye	5540 Gulf of Mexico Dr	383-3633
15 South Ristorante	15 S Blvd of Presidents	708-8312
Fast N Fresh	8105 Cooper Creek	315-4500
Fast N Fresh	32 S Osprey Ave	702-2900
Fast N Fresh	8138 Lkewood Main St	462-2650
Flavio's Brick Oven	5239 Ocean Blvd	349-0995
Fleming's Steakhouse	2001 Siesta Dr	358-9463
Fresh Start Cafe	630 Orange Ave	373-1242
Gecko's Grill & Pub	4870 S Tamiami Trl	923-8896
Gecko's Grill & Pub	1900 Hillview St	953-2929
Gecko's Grill & Pub	5588 Palmer Crossing	923-6061
Gecko's Grill & Pub	351 N Cattlemen Rd	378-0077
Gentile Cheesesteaks	7523 S Tamiami Trl	926-0441
Gilligan's Island Bar	5253 Ocean Blvd	346-8122
The Grasshopper	7253 S Tamiami Trl	923-3688
Half Shell Seafood Hse	5231 University Pkwy	952-9400
Harry's Continental Kit.	525 St Judes Dr	383-0777

Restaurant Name	Address	Phone #
Heaven Ham/Devil Dogs	2647 Mall Dr	923-2514
Hillview Grill	1920 Hillview Ave	952-0045
Hob Nob Drive-In	1701 Washington Blvd	955-5001
Hot Diggity Dog	5666 Swift Rd	922-8018
The Hub Baha Grill	5148 Ocean Blvd	349-6800
Hyde Park Steakhouse	35 S Lemon Ave	366-7781
Il Panificio	1703 Main St	366-5570
Il Panificio	6630 Gateway Ave	921-5570
Indigenous	239 Links Ave	706-4740
Jack Dusty	1111 Ritz-Carlton Dr	309-2266
Joey D's Chicago Eatery	3811 Kenny Dr	376-8900
Joey D's Chicago Eatery	211 N. Tamiami Trl	364-9900
JoTo Japanese Rest.	5218 Ocean Blvd	346-8366
Jpan Sushi Bar	3 Paradise Plaza	954-5726
Kacey's Seafood & More	4904 Fruitville Rd	378-3644
Karl Ehmer's Alpine	4520 S. Tamiami Trl	922-3797
Kazu 2.0	6566 Gateway Ave	922-5459
Knick's Tavern & Grill	1818 S Osprey Ave	955-7761
Kumo Japanese	5231 University Pkwy	355-5866
The Lazy Lobster	7602 N Lockwood Rg	351-5515
The Lazy Lobster	3550 Gulf of Mexico Dr	383-0440
LeLu Coffee Lounge	5251 Ocean Blvd	346-5358
Libby's Cafe + Bar	1917 Osprey Ave	487-7300
Lido Beach Grille	700 Ben Franklin Dr	388-2161
The Lobster Pot	5157 Ocean Blvd	349-2323
Lolita Tartine	1419 5th St	952-3172
Louies Modern	1289 N Palm Ave	552-9688
Lynches Pub & Grub	19 N Blvd of Pres	388-5550

Restaurant Name	Address	Phone #
MacAllisters Grill	8110 Lakewood Main	359-2424
Made	1990 Main St	953-2900
Madfish Grill	4059 Cattlemen Rd	377-3474
Main Bar Sandwich Shp	1944 Main St	955-8733
Main Street Trattoria	8131 Lakewood Main	907-1518
Maison Blanche	2605 Gulf of Mexico Dr	383-8088
Mandeville Beer Garden	428 N Lemon Ave	954-8688
Marcello's Ristorante	4155 S. Tamiami Trl	921-6794
Marina Jack's	2 Marina Plaza	365-4243
Mar-Vista Restaurant	760 Broadway St	383-2391
Mattison's City Grille	1 N Lemon Ave	330-0440
Mattison's Forty One	7275 S Tamiami Trl	921-3400
Matto Matto	543 S Pineapple Ave	444-7196
Mediterraneo	1970 Main St	365-4122
Melange	1568 Main St	953-7111
Mi Pueblo	4436 Bee Ridge Rd	379-2880
Mi Pueblo	4804 Tuttle Ave	359-9303
Mi Tierra Restaurant	1068 N Washington	330-0196
Michael John's	1040 Carlton Arms Blv	747-8032
Michael's On East	1212 East Ave	366-0007
Michelle's Brown Bag	1819 Main St	365-5858
Miguel's	6631 Midnight Pass	349-4024
Miller's Ale House	3800 Kenny Dr	378-8888
Mozaic	1377 Main St	951-6272
Mozzarella Fella	1668 Main St	366-7600
Munchies 420 Cafe	6639 Superior Ave	929-9393
Muse At The Ringling	5401 Bay Shore Rd	360-7390
Nancy's Bar-B-Que	301 S Pineapple Ave	366-2271

Restaurant Name	Address	Phone #
New Pass Grill	1505 Ken Thompson	388-3119
Oasis Cafe	3542 S Osprey Ave	957-1214
Off The Hook Seafood	6630 Gateway Ave	923-5570
Oh Mamma Mia!	2324 Gulf Gate Dr	706-2821
Old Packinghouse Cafe	987 S Packinghouse Rd	371-9358
The Old Salty Dog	5023 Ocean Blvd	349-0158
The Old Salty Dog	160 Ken Thompson Pk	388-4311
The Old Salty Dog	1485 S Tamiami Trl.	483-1000
Ophelia's on the Bay	9105 Midnight Pass	349-2212
Ortygia	1418 13th Street W	741-8646
Owen's Fish Camp	516 Burns Ct	951-6936
3.14 Pi Craft Beer	5263 Ocean Blvd	346-1188
Pacific Rim	1859 Hillview St	330-8071
Patrick's 1481	1481 Main St	955-1481
Pattigeorge's	7120 Gulf of Mexico Dr	383-5111
Phillippi Creek Oyster	5363 S Tamiami Trl	925-4444
Pho Cali	1578 Main St	955-2683
Pier 22	1200 1st Avenue W	748-8087
Pino's	3800 S Tamiami Trl	366-1440
Polo Bar & Grill	10670 Boardwalk Lp	782-0899
Pomona Bistro	481 N Orange Ave	706-1677
Primo! Ristorante	8076 N Tamiami Trl	359-3690
Pub 32	8383 S Tamiami Trl	952-3070
Queen Of Sheba	34195 N Tamiami Trl	359-8000
Rev-el-ry Pub & Grill	3005 University Pkwy	355-1218
Riverhouse Reef Grill	995 Riverside Dr	729-0616
Roadside Rib Shack	2045 Bahia Vista St.	330-9597
Roast Restaurant & Bar	1296 First St	953-1971

Restaurant Name	Address	Phone #
Roessler's	2033 Vamo Way	966-5688
Rosati's Pizza	935 N Beneva Rd	953-1802
Rosebud's Steakhouse	2215 S Tamiami Trl	918-8771
Roy's Restaurant	2001 Siesta Dr	952-0109
The Russian House	6115 S Tamiami Trl	735-1151
Ruth's Chris Steakhouse	6700 S Tamiami Trl	942-9442
62 Bistrot	1962 Hillview St	954-1011
Saltwater Cafe	1071 N Tamiami Trl	488-3775
Salute! Ristorante	23 N Lemon Ave	365-1020
The Sandbar	100 Spring Ave	778-0444
Sarasota Brewing Co	6607 Gateway Ave	925-2337
Sardinia	5770 S Tamiami Trl	702-8582
Selva Grill	1345 Main St	362-4427
Senor Siesta	5110 Ocean Blvd	349-0818
Shakespeare's Eng Pub	3550 S Osprey Ave	364-5938
Shaner's Pizza	6500 Superior Ave	927-2708
The Shamrock	2257 Ringling Blvd	952-1730
Sharkey's on the Pier	1600 Harbor Dr S	488-1456
Shore Diner	465 John Ringling Blvd	296-0303
Siesta Key Oyster Bar	5238 Ocean Blvd	346-5443
S'Macks Burgers	2407 Bee Ridge Rd	922-7673
Social Eatery & Bar	1219 First St	444-7072
Sol Meyer's NY Deli	1473 Main St.	955-3354
Solorzano's	6516 Superior Ave	906-9444
Solorzano Bros. Pizza	3604 Webber St	926-4276
Solorzano Bros. Pizza	5251 Ocean Blvd	346-5358
Square 1 Burgers	1737 S Tamiami Trl	870-8111
The Starlite Room	1001 Cocoanut Ave	702-5613

Restaurant Name	Address	Phone #
State St Eating House	1533 State St	951-1533
Station 400	400 Lemon Ave	906-1400
Station 400	8215 Lakewood Main	907-0648
Stottlemeyer's Smokehs	19 East Rd.	312-5969
Sun Garden Cafe	210 Avenida Madera	346-7170
Surf Shack	326 John Ringling Blvd	960-1122
The Table Creekside	5365 S Tamiami Trl	921-9465
Tandoor	8453 Cooper Creek	926-3070
Taste of Asia	4413 S Tamiami Trl	923-2742
Tasty Home Cookin'	3854 S Tuttle Ave	921-4969
Thailand Restaurant	2238 Gulf Gate Dr	927-8424
Toasted Mango Cafe	430 N. Tamiami Trl.	388-7728
Tommy Bahama Cafe	300 John Ringling Blvd	388-2888
Tony's Chicago Beef	6569 Superior Ave	922-7979
Tony's Chicago Beef	2117 Siesta Dr	993-1531
Turtle's	8875 Midnight Pass	346-2207
Two Senorita's	1355 Main St	366-1618
Veg	2164 Gulf Gate Dr	312-6424
Venezia	373 St. Armands Cir	388-1400
Village Cafe	5133 Ocean Blvd	349-2822
Walt's Fish Market	4144 S Tamiami Trl	921-4605
Waterfront	7660 S Tamiami Trl	921-1916
Word of Mouth	6604 Gateway Ave	925-2400
Word of Mouth	711 S Osprey Ave	365-1800
Yo Sushi!	140 Univ. Town Ctr Dr	313-7091
Yoder's Restaurant	3434 Bahia Vista	955-7771
Yume Sushi	1532 Main St	363-0604
Yummy House	3232 N Tamiami Trl	351-1688

AMERICAN		
Restaurant Name	**Address**	**Phone #**
Baker & Wife	2157 Siesta Dr	960-1765
Beach Bistro	6600 Gulf Dr N	778-6444
Bijou Cafe	1287 First St	366-8111
Blase Cafe	5263 Ocean Blvd	349-9822
Blue Rooster	1524 4th St	388-7539
Boatyard Waterfront Grill	1500 Stickney Pt Rd	921-6200
The Breakfast House	1817 Fruitville Rd.	366-6860
The Broken Egg	4031 Clark Rd	922-2868
Burns Court Cafe	401 S Pineapple Ave	312-6633
Cafe In The Park	2010 Adams Ln	361-3032
Cafe Venice	116 W. Venice Ave.	484-1855
Carmel Cafe	8433 Cooper Crk Blvd	893-5955
Cha Cha Coconuts	417 St Armands Cir	388-3300
Clayton's Siesta Grille	1256 Old Stickney Pt	349-2800
Coffee Carrousel	1644 Main St	365-2826
The Cottage	153 Avenida Messina	312-9300
Currents	1000 Blvd of the Arts	953-1234
Der Dutchman	3713 Bahia Vista	955-8007
Daiquiri Deck Raw Bar	5250 Ocean Blvd	349-8697
Daiquiri Deck Raw Bar	325 John Ringling Blvd	388-3325
Daiquiri Deck Raw Bar	300 W Venice Ave	488-0649
Derek's Rustic Coastal	5516 Manatee Ave	794-1100
Dutch Valley Restaurant	6731 S Tamiami Trl	924-1770
Duval's New World Cafe	1435 Main St	312-4001
Eat Here	240 Avenida Madera	346-7800
Euphemia Haye	5540 Gulf of Mexico Dr	383-3633
Fast N Fresh	8105 Cooper Creek	315-4500

AMERICAN		
Restaurant Name	Address	Phone #
Fresh Start Cafe	630 Orange Ave	373-1242
Gecko's Grill & Pub	4870 S Tamiami Trl	923-8896
Gecko's Grill & Pub	1900 Hillview St	953-2929
Gecko's Grill & Pub	5588 Palmer Crossing	923-6061
Gecko's Grill & Pub	351 N Cattlemen Rd	378-0077
Gilligan's Island Bar	5253 Ocean Blvd	346-8122
Harry's Continental Kit.	525 St Judes Dr	383-0777
Hillview Grill	1920 Hillview Ave	952-0045
Hob Nob Drive-In	1701 Washington Blvd	955-5001
Hot Diggity Dog	5666 Swift Rd	922-8018
The Hub Baha Grill	5148 Ocean Blvd	349-6800
Indigenous	239 Links Ave	706-4740
Jack Dusty	1111 Ritz-Carlton Dr	309-2266
Joey D's Chicago Eatery	3811 Kenny Dr	376-8900
Kacey's Seafood & More	4904 Fruitville Rd	378-3644
Knick's Tavern & Grill	1818 S Osprey Ave	955-7761
LeLu Coffee Lounge	5251 Ocean Blvd	346-5358
Libby's Cafe + Bar	1917 Osprey Ave	487-7300
Lido Beach Grille	700 Ben Franklin Dr	388-2161
Louies Modern	1289 N Palm Ave	552-9688
Made	1990 Main St	953-2900
Mandeville Beer Garden	428 N Lemon Ave	954-8688
Marcello's Ristorante	4155 S Tamiami Trl	921-6794
Mar-Vista Restaurant	760 Broadway St	383-2391
Mattison's City Grille	1 N Lemon Ave	330-0440
Mattison's Forty One	7275 S Tamiami Trl	921-3400
Melange	1568 Main St	953-7111
Michael John's	1040 Carlton Arms Blv	747-8032

AMERICAN		
Restaurant Name	**Address**	**Phone #**
Michael's On East	1212 East Ave	366-0007
Miller's Ale House	3800 Kenny Dr	378-8888
Mozaic	1377 Main St	951-6272
Munchies 420 Cafe	6639 Superior Ave	929-9393
Muse At The Ringling	5401 Bay Shore Rd	360-7390
Nancy's Bar-B-Que	301 S. Pineapple Ave	366-2271
New Pass Grill	1505 Ken Thompson	388-3119
Oasis Cafe	3542 S Osprey Ave	957-1214
Old Packinghouse Cafe	987 S Packinghouse Rd	371-9358
The Old Salty Dog	5023 Ocean Blvd	349-0158
The Old Salty Dog	160 Ken Thompson Pk	388-4311
Ophelia's on the Bay	9105 Midnight Pass	349-2212
Patrick's 1481	1481 Main St	955-1481
Pattigeorge's	7120 Gulf of Mexico Dr	383-5111
Polo Bar & Grill	10670 Boardwalk Lp	782-0899
Pomona Bistro	481 N Orange Ave	706-1677
Rev-el-ry Pub & Grill	3005 University Pkwy	355-1218
Roadside Rib Shack	2045 Bahia Vista St.	330-9597
Roast Restaurant & Bar	1296 First St	953-1971
The Sandbar	100 Spring Ave	778-0444
Sarasota Brewing Co	6607 Gateway Ave	925-2337
Savory Street Cafe	411 N Orange Ave	312-4027
Sharkey's on the Pier	1600 Harbor Dr S	488-1456
Shore Diner	465 John Ringling Blvd	296-0303
Siesta Key Oyster Bar	5238 Ocean Blvd	346-5443
S'Macks Burgers	2407 Bee Ridge Rd	922-7673
Social Eatery & Bar	1219 First St	444-7072

AMERICAN		
Restaurant Name	**Address**	**Phone #**
Square 1 Burgers	1737 S Tamiami Trl	870-8111
State St Eating House	1533 State St	951-1533
The Starlite Room	1001 Cocoanut Ave	702-5613
Station 400	400 Lemon Ave	906-1400
Station 400	8215 Lakewood Main	907-0648
Stottlemeyer's Smokehs	19 East Rd.	312-5969
Surf Shack	326 John Ringling Blvd	960-1122
Sun Garden Cafe	210 Avenida Madera	346-7170
The Table Creekside	5365 S Tamiami Trl	921-9465
Tasty Home Cookin'	3854 S Tuttle Ave	921-4969
Tommy Bahama Cafe	300 John Ringling Blvd	388-2888
Tony's Chicago Beef	6569 Superior Ave	922-7979
Turtle's	8875 Midnight Pass	346-2207
Veg	2164 Gulf Gate Dr	312-6424
Village Cafe	5133 Ocean Blvd	349-2822
Waterfront	7660 S Tamiami Trl	921-1916
Word of Mouth	6604 Gateway Ave	925-2400
Word of Mouth	711 S Osprey Ave	365-1800
Yoder's Restaurant	3434 Bahia Vista	955-7771

ASIAN		
DaRuMa Japanese	5459 Fruitville Rd	342-6600
Drunken Poet Cafe	1572 Main St	955-8404
JoTo Japanese Rest.	5218 Ocean Blvd	346-8366
Jpan Sushi Bar	3 Paradise Plaza	954-5726
Kazu 2.0	6566 Gateway Ave	922-5459
Kumo Japanese	5231 University Pkwy	355-5866

ASIAN		
Pacific Rim	1859 Hillview St	330-8071
Pho Cali	1578 Main St	955-2683
Roy's Restaurant	2001 Siesta Dr	952-0109
Taste of Asia	4413 S Tamiami Trl	923-2742
Thailand Restaurant	2238 Gulf Gate Dr	927-8424
Yo Sushi!	140 Univ. Town Ctr Dr	313-7091
Yume Sushi	1532 Main St	363-0604
Yummy House	3232 N Tamiami Trl	351-1688

CUBAN, MEXICAN & SPANISH		
Restaurant Name	Address	Phone #
The Columbia	411 St Armands Cir	388-3987
El Toro Bravo	2720 Stickney Pt	924-0006
The Grasshopper	7253 S Tamiami Trl	923-3688
Mi Pueblo	4436 Bee Ridge Rd	379-2880
Mi Pueblo	4804 Tuttle Ave	359-9303
Mi Tierra Restaurant	1068 N Washington	330-0196
Senor Siesta	5110 Ocean Blvd	349-0818

DELI		
Anna's Deli	6535 Midnight Pass	349-4888
Anna's Deli	8207 Tourist Ctr Dr	893-5908
Corkscrew Deli	4982 S Tamiami Trl	925-3955
Gentile Cheesesteaks	7523 S Tamiami Trl	926-0441
Heaven Ham/Devil Dogs	2647 Mall Dr	923-2514
Main Bar Sandwich Shp	1944 Main St	955-8733
Michelle's Brown Bag	1819 Main St	365-5858
Mozzarella Fella	1668 Main St	366-7600
Sol Meyer's NY Deli	1473 Main St.	955-3354

ENGLISH, IRISH & SCOTTISH		
Lynches Pub & Grub	19 N Blvd of Pres	388-5550
MacAllisters Grill	8110 Lakewood Main	359-2424
Pub 32	8383 S Tamiami Trl	952-3070
Shakespeare's Eng Pub	3550 S Osprey Ave	364-5938
The Shamrock	2257 Ringling Blvd	952-1730

FRENCH		
Restaurant Name	Address	Phone #
Bonjour French Cafe	5214 Ocean Blvd	346-0600
C'est La Vie!	1553 Main St	906-9575
Lolita Tartine	1419 5th St	952-3172
Maison Blanche	2605 Gulf of Mexico Dr	383-8088
Miguel's	6631 Midnight Pass	349-4024
62 Bistrot	1962 Hillview St	954-1011

GREEK		
Apollonia Grill	8235 Cooper Creek	359-4816
Blu Kouzina	25 N Blvd of Pres.	388-2619
El Greco Cafe	1592 Main St	365-2234

INDIAN		
Chutney's, Etc.	1944 Hillview Dr	954-4444
Curry Station	1303 N Washington	312-6264
Tandoor	8453 Cooper Creek	926-3070

ITALIAN		
Adriatico	6606 Superior Ave	922-3080
Amore By Andrea	555 Bay Isles Pkwy	383-1111
Andrea's	2085 Siesta Dr	951-9200

ITALIAN		
Restaurant Name	Address	Phone #
Cafe Don Giovanni	5610 Gulf of Mexico Dr	383-0013
Cafe Epicure	1298 Main St	366-5648
Cafe Gabbiano	5104 Ocean Blvd	349-1423
Cafe L'Europe	431 St Armands Cir	388-4415
Caragiulos	69 S Palm Ave	951-0866
Clasico Cafe + Bar	1341 Main St	957-0700
Cosimo's Trattoria	3501 Palmer Crossing	922-7999
Demetrio's Restaurant	4410 S Tamiami Trl	922-1585
Dolce Italia	6606 Superior Ave	921-7007
15 South Ristorante	15 S Blvd of Presidents	708-8312
Flavio's Brick Oven	5239 Ocean Blvd	349-0995
Il Panificio	1703 Main St	366-5570
Il Panificio	6630 Gateway Ave	921-5570
Main Street Trattoria	8131 Lakewood Main	907-1518
Marcello's Ristorante	4155 S Tamiami Trl	921-6794
Matto Matto	543 S Pineapple Ave	444-7196
Mediterraneo	1970 Main St	365-4122
Oh Mamma Mia!	2324 Gulf Gate Dr	706-2821
Piccolo Italian Market	6518 Gateway Ave	923-2202
Pino's	3800 S Tamiami Trl	366-1440
Primo! Ristorante	8076 N Tamiami Trl	359-3690
Rosati's Pizza	935 N Beneva Rd	953-1802
Salute! Ristorante	23 N Lemon Ave	365-1020
Sardinia	5770 S Tamiami Trl	702-8582
Shaner's Pizza	6500 Superior Ave	927-2708
Solorzano's	6516 Superior Ave	906-9444
Solorzano Bros. Pizza	3604 Webber St	926-4276
Solorzano Bros. Pizza	5251 Ocean Blvd	346-5358

SEAFOOD		
Restaurant Name	Address	Phone #
Anna Maria Oyster Bar	6906 14th St W	758-7880
Anna Maria Oyster Bar	6696 Cortez Rd	792-0077
Anna Maria Oyster Bar	1525 51st Ave E	721-7773
Barnacle Bills Seafood	1526 Main St	365-6800
Barnacle Bills Seafood	5050 N. Tamiami Trl	355-7700
Big Water Fish Market	6641 Midhight Pass	554-8101
Capt. Brian's Seafood	8421 N Tamiami Trl	351-4491
Capt. Curt's Oyster Bar	1200 Old Stickney Pt	349-3885
Casey Key Fish House	801 Blackburn Pt Rd	966-1901
Crab & Fin	420 St. Armands Cir	388-3964
The Crow's Nest	1968 Tarpon Ctr Dr	484-9551
Dry Dock Waterfront	412 Gulf of Mexico Dr	383-0102
Half Shell Seafood Hse	5231 University Pkwy	952-9400
The Lazy Lobster	7602 N Lockwood Rg	351-5515
The Lazy Lobster	3550 Gulf of Mexico Dr	383-0440
The Lobster Pot	5157 Ocean Blvd	349-2323
Madfish Grill	4059 Cattlemen Rd	377-3474
Mar-Vista Restaurant	760 Broadway St	383-2391
Marina Jack's	2 Marina Plaza	365-4243
Off The Hook Seafood	6630 Gateway Ave	923-5570
Owen's Fish Camp	516 Burns Ct	951-6936
Phillippi Creek Oyster	5363 S Tamiami Trl	925-4444
Pier 22	1200 1st Avenue W	748-8087
Riverhouse Reef Grill	995 Riverside Dr	729-0616
Saltwater Cafe	1071 N Tamiami Trl	488-3775
Walt's Fish Market	4144 S Tamiami Trl	921-4605

STEAKHOUSE		
Restaurant Name	**Address**	**Phone #**
Fleming's Steakhouse	2001 Siesta Dr	358-9463
Hyde Park Steakhouse	35 S Lemon Ave	366-7781
Karl Ehmer's Alpine	4520 S. Tamiami Trl	922-3797
Rosebud's Steakhouse	2215 S Tamiami Trl	918-8771
Ruth's Chris Steakhouse	6700 S Tamiami Trl	942-9442

SARASOTA FOOD EVENTS

FORKS & CORKS
WHEN: January, 29-31st
WHAT: Sponsored by the Sarasota-Manatee Originals it's an all out food fest. Wine dinners, seminars and of course the Grand Tasting.
INFO: www.dineoriginal.com/forksandcorks

FLORIDA WINEFEST & AUCTION
WHEN: March, 17-20th
WHAT: This popular charity event has been providing needed help to local children's programs for the past 24 years. The Grand Tasting Brunch and Charity Auction are a highlight of the year.
INFO: floridawinefest.org

SAVOR SARASOTA RESTAURANT WEEK
WHEN: June, 1-14th
WHAT: This super popular food event actually spans two full weeks. It features lots of popular restaurants and showcases 3 course menus.
INFO: www.savorsarasota.com

ANNA MARIA, BRADENTON & PALMETTO		
Restaurant Name	**Address**	**Phone #**
Beach Bistro	6600 Gulf Dr N	778-6444
Derek's Rustic Coastal	5516 Manatee Ave	794-1100

ANNA MARIA, BRADENTON & PALMETTO		
Restaurant Name	Address	Phone #
Michael John's	1040 Carlton Arms Blv	747-8032
Ortygia	1418 13th Street W	741-8646
Pier 22	1200 1st Avenue W	748-8087
Riverhouse Reef Grill	995 Riverside Dr	729-0616

DOWNTOWN		
Artisan Cheese Co.	1310 Main St	951-7860
Barnacle Bills Seafood	1526 Main St	365-6800
Bijou Cafe	1287 First St	366-8111
Blue Rooster	1524 4th St	388-7539
The Breakfast House	1817 Fruitville Rd.	366-6860
Burns Court Cafe	401 S Pineapple Ave	312-6633
Cafe Epicure	1298 Main St	366-5648
Caragiulos	69 S Palm Ave	951-0866
C'est La Vie!	1553 Main St	906-9575
Clasico Cafe + Bar	1341 Main St	957-0700
Coffee Carrousel	1644 Main St	365-2826
Currents	1000 Blvd of the Arts	953-1234
Curry Station	1303 N Washington	312-6264
Drunken Poet Cafe	1572 Main St	955-8404
Duval's New World Cafe	1435 Main St	312-4001
El Greco Cafe	1592 Main St	365-2234
Fresh Start Cafe	630 Orange Ave	373-1242
Hyde Park Steakhouse	35 S Lemon Ave	366-7781
Il Panificio	1703 Main St	366-5570
Indigenous	239 Links Ave	706-4740
Jack Dusty	1111 Ritz-Carlton Dr	309-2266
Lolita Tartine	1419 5th St	952-3172

DOWNTOWN		
Restaurant Name	**Address**	**Phone #**
Louies Modern	1289 N Palm Ave	552-9688
Made	1990 Main St	953-2900
Main Bar Sandwich Shp	1944 Main St	955-8733
Mandeville Beer Garden	428 N Lemon Ave	954-8688
Marina Jack's	2 Marina Plaza	365-4243
Mattison's City Grille	1 N Lemon Ave	330-0440
Matto Matto	543 S Pineapple Ave	444-7196
Mediterraneo	1970 Main St	365-4122
Melange	1568 Main St	953-7111
Mi Tierra Restaurant	1068 N Washington	330-0196
Michelle's Brown Bag	1819 Main St	365-5858
Mozaic	1377 Main St	951-6272
Mozzarella Fella	1668 Main St	366-7600
Nancy's Bar-B-Que	301 S Pineapple Ave	366-2271
Owen's Fish Camp	516 Burns Ct	951-6936
Patrick's 1481	1481 Main St	955-1481
Pho Cali	1578 Main St	955-2683
Pomona Bistro	481 N Orange Ave	706-1677
Roast Restaurant & Bar	1296 First St	953-1971
Salute! Ristorante	23 N Lemon Ave	365-1020
Savory Street Cafe	411 N Orange Ave	312-4027
Selva Grill	1345 Main St	362-4427
The Shamrock	2257 Ringling Blvd	952-1730
Social Eatery & Bar	1219 First St	444-7072
Sol Meyer's NY Deli	1473 Main St.	955-3354
State St Eating House	1533 State St	951-1533
The Starlite Room	1001 Cocoanut Ave	702-5613
Station 400	400 Lemon Ave	906-1400

DOWNTOWN		
Restaurant Name	**Address**	**Phone #**
Two Senorita's	1355 Main St	366-1618
Yume Sushi	1532 Main St	363-0604
GULF GATE		
Adriatico	6606 Superior Ave	922-3080
Dolce Italia	6606 Superior Ave	921-7007
Heaven Ham/Devil Dogs	2647 Mall Dr	923-2514
Kazu 2.0	6566 Gateway Ave	922-5459
Munchies 420 Cafe	6639 Superior Ave	929-9393
Off The Hook Seafood	6630 Gateway Ave	923-5570
Oh Mamma Mia!	2324 Gulf Gate Dr	706-2821
Piccolo Italian Market	6518 Gateway Ave	923-2202
Sarasota Brewing Co	6607 Gateway Ave	925-2337
Shaner's Pizza	6500 Superior Ave	927-2708
Solorzano's	6516 Superior Ave	906-9444
Thailand Restaurant	2238 Gulf Gate Dr	927-8424
Tony's Chicago Beef	6569 Superior Ave	922-7979
Veg	2164 Gulf Gate Dr	312-6424
Word of Mouth	6604 Gateway Ave	925-2400

LONGBOAT KEY		
Amore By Andrea	555 Bay Isles Pkwy	383-1111
Cafe Don Giovanni	5610 Gulf of Mexico Dr	383-0013
Dry Dock Waterfront	412 Gulf of Mexico Dr	383-0102
Euphemia Haye	5540 Gulf of Mexico Dr	383-3633
Harry's Continental Kit.	525 St Judes Dr	383-0777
Maison Blanche	2605 Gulf of Mexico Dr	383-8088
Mar-Vista Restaurant	760 Broadway St	383-2391
Pattigeorge's	7120 Gulf of Mexico Dr	383-5111

LAKEWOOD RANCH & UNIVERSITY PARK

Restaurant Name	Address	Phone #
Apollonia Grill	8235 Cooper Creek	359-4816
Carmel Cafe	8433 Cooper Crk Blvd	893-5955
Fast N Fresh	8105 Cooper Creek	315-4500
Half Shell Seafood Hse	5231 University Pkwy	952-9400
Kumo Japanese	5231 University Pkwy	355-5866
Fast N Fresh	8105 Cooper Creek	315-4500
Half Shell Seafood Hse	5231 University Pkwy	952-9400
Kumo Japanese	5231 University Pkwy	355-5866
Polo Bar & Grill	10670 Boardwalk Lp	782-0899
Rev-el-ry Pub & Grill	3005 University Pkwy	355-1218
Tandoor	8453 Cooper Creek	926-3070

NORTH TAMIAMI TRAIL

Capt. Brian's Seafood	8421 N Tamiami Trl	351-4491
Hob Nob Drive-In	1701 Washington Blvd	955-5001
Primo! Ristorante	8076 N Tamiami Trl	359-3690
Muse At The Ringling	5401 Bay Shore Rd	360-7390
Queen Of Sheba	34195 N Tamiami Trl	359-8000
Yummy House	3232 N Tamiami Trl	351-1688

ST. ARMANDS KEY

Blu Kouzina	25 N Blvd of Pres.	388-2619
Cafe L'Europe	431 St Armands Cir	388-4415
Cha Cha Coconuts	417 St Armands Cir	388-3300
The Columbia	411 St Armands Cir	388-3987
Crab & Fin	420 St. Armands Cir	388-3964
15 South Ristorante	15 S Blvd of Presidents	708-8312
Lynches Pub & Grub	19 N Blvd of Pres	388-5550

ST. ARMANDS KEY		
Restaurant Name	**Address**	**Phone #**
Shore Diner	465 John Ringling Blvd	296-0303
Surf Shack	326 John Ringling Blvd	960-1122
Tommy Bahama Cafe	300 John Ringling Blvd	388-2888

SIESTA KEY		
Anna's Deli	6535 Midnight Pass	349-4888
Big Water Fish Market	6641 Midhight Pass	554-8101
Blase Cafe	5263 Ocean Blvd	349-9822
Blu Que Island Grill	149 Avenida Messina	346-0738
Bonjour French Cafe	5214 Ocean Blvd	346-0600
Cafe Gabbiano	5104 Ocean Blvd	349-1423
Capt. Curt's Oyster Bar	1200 Old Stickney Pt	349-3885
Clayton's Siesta Grille	1256 Old Stickney Pt	349-2800
Daiquiri Deck Raw Bar	5250 Ocean Blvd	349-8697
The Cottage	153 Avenida Messina	312-9300
Eat Here	240 Avenida Madera	346-7800
Flavio's Brick Oven	5239 Ocean Blvd	349-0995
Gilligan's Island Bar	5253 Ocean Blvd	346-8122
The Hub Baha Grill	5148 Ocean Blvd	349-6800
JoTo Japanese Rest.	5218 Ocean Blvd	346-8366
LeLu Coffee Lounge	5251 Ocean Blvd	346-5358
The Lobster Pot	5157 Ocean Blvd	349-2323
Miguel's	6631 Midnight Pass	349-4024
The Old Salty Dog	5023 Ocean Blvd	349-0158
Ophelia's on the Bay	9105 Midnight Pass	349-2212
Ophelia's on the Bay	9105 Midnight Pass	349-2212
3.14 Pi Craft Beer	5263 Ocean Blvd	346-1188
Senor Siesta	5110 Ocean Blvd	349-0818

SIESTA KEY		
Restaurant Name	**Address**	**Phone #**
Siesta Key Oyster Bar	5238 Ocean Blvd	346-5443
Solorzano Bros. Pizza	5251 Ocean Blvd	346-5358
Sun Garden Cafe	210 Avenida Madera	346-7170
Toasted Mango Cafe	6621 Midnight Pass	552-6485
Turtle's	8875 Midnight Pass	346-2207
Village Cafe	5133 Ocean Blvd	349-2822

SOUTH TAMIAMI TRAIL		
Corkscrew Deli	4982 S Tamiami Trl	925-3955
Demetrio's Restaurant	4410 S Tamiami Trl	922-1585
Dutch Valley Restaurant	6731 S Tamiami Trl	924-1770
Gecko's Grill & Pub	4870 S Tamiami Trl	923-8896
Gentile Cheesesteaks	7523 S Tamiami Trl	926-0441
The Grasshopper	7253 S Tamiami Trl	923-3688
Karl Ehmer's Alpine	4520 S. Tamiami Trl	922-3797
Marcello's Ristorante	4155 S Tamiami Trl	921-6794
Mattison's Forty One	7275 S Tamiami Trl	921-3400
Phillippi Creek Oyster	5363 S Tamiami Trl	925-4444
Pub 32	8383 S Tamiami Trl	952-3070
Roessler's	2033 Vamo Way	966-5688
Rosebud's Steakhouse	2215 S Tamiami Trl	918-8771
The Russian House	6115 S Tamiami Trl	735-1151
Ruth's Chris Steakhouse	6700 S Tamiami Trl	942-9442
Sardinia	5770 S Tamiami Trl	702-8582
Square 1 Burgers	1737 S Tamiami Trl	870-8111
The Table Creekside	5365 S Tamiami Trl	921-9465
Taste of Asia	4413 S Tamiami Trl	923-2742
Walt's Fish Market	4144 S Tamiami Trl	921-4605

SOUTH TAMIAMI TRAIL		
Restaurant Name	**Address**	**Phone #**
Waterfront	7660 S Tamiami Trl	921-1916

SOUTHSIDE VILLAGE		
Restaurant Name	**Address**	**Phone #**
Chutney's, Etc.	1944 Hillview Dr	954-4444
Hillview Grill	1920 Hillview Ave	952-0045
Knick's Tavern & Grill	1818 S Osprey Ave	955-7761
Libby's Cafe + Bar	1917 Osprey Ave	487-7300
Pacific Rim	1859 Hillview St	330-8071
62 Bistrot	1962 Hillview St	954-1011

SOUTHGATE		
Andrea's	2085 Siesta Dr	951-9200
Baker & Wife	2157 Siesta Dr	960-1765
Fleming's Steakhouse	2001 Siesta Dr	358-9463
Roy's Restaurant	2001 Siesta Dr	952-0109

UNIVERSITY TOWN CENTER (UTC)		
Brio Tuscan Grille	190 Univ. Town Ctr Dr	702-9102
Burger & Beer Joint	160 Univ. Town Ctr Dr	702-9915
The Capital Grille	180 Univ. Town Ctr Dr	256-3647
Cheesecake Factory	130 Univ. Town Ctr Dr	256-3760
Kona Grill	150 Univ. Town Ctr Dr	256-8005
Rise Pies Pizza	140 Univ. Town Ctr Dr	702-9920
Seasons 52	170 Univ. Town Ctr Dr	702-9652
Sophies	120 Univ. Town Ctr Dr	444-3077
Yo Sushi!	140 Univ. Town Ctr Dr	313-7091

LIVE MUSIC		
Restaurant Name	**Address**	**Phone #**
Blase Cafe	5263 Ocean Blvd	349-9822
Blu Que Island Grill	149 Avenida Messina	346-0738
Blue Rooster	1524 4th St	388-7539
Boatyard Waterfront Grill	1500 Stickney Pt Rd	921-6200
Capt. Curt's Oyster Bar	1200 Old Stickney Pt	349-3885
Casey Key Fish House	801 Blackburn Pt Rd	966-1901
Clasico Cafe + Bar	1341 Main St	957-0700
Gilligan's Island Bar	5253 Ocean Blvd	346-8122
Lido Beach Grille	700 Ben Franklin Dr	388-2161
Marina Jack's	2 Marina Plaza	365-4243
Mattison's City Grille	1 N Lemon Ave	330-0440
Mattison's Forty One	7275 S Tamiami Trl	921-3400
Matto Matto	543 S Pineapple Ave	951-2600
Michael's On East	1212 East Ave	366-0007
Old Packinghouse Cafe	987 S Packinghouse	371-9358
Sharkey's on the Pier	1600 Harbor Dr S	488-1456
Siesta Key Oyster Bar	5238 Ocean Blvd	346-5443
Walt's Fish Market	4144 S Tamiami Trl	921-4605

CATERING		
BeachHouse Restaurant	200 Gulf Dr N	779-2222
Cafe L'Europe	431 St Armands Cir	388-4415
Chutney's, Etc.	1944 Hillview Dr	954-4444
Cosimo's Trattoria	3501 Palmer Crossing	922-7999
Currents	1000 Blvd of the Arts	953-1234
Daiquiri Deck Raw Bar	5250 Ocean Blvd	349-8697
Gecko's Grill & Pub	4870 S Tamiami Trl	923-8896
Harry's Continental Kit.	525 St Judes Dr	383-0777

CATERING		
Restaurant Name	**Address**	**Phone #**
Libby's Cafe + Bar	1917 Osprey Ave	487-7300
Louies Modern	1289 N Palm Ave	552-9688
Mattison's Forty One	7275 S Tamiami Trl	921-3400
Michael's On East	1212 East Ave	366-0007
Nancy's Bar-B-Que	301 S Pineapple Ave	366-2271
Nellie's Deli & Market	15 S Beneva Rd	924-2705
Pattigeorge's	7120 Gulf of Mexico Dr	383-5111
Polo Bar & Grill	10670 Boardwalk Lp	782-0899
Sun Garden Cafe	210 Avenida Madera	346-7170
Village Cafe	5133 Ocean Blvd	349-2822

ONLINE RESERVATIONS		
Antoine's Restaurant	5020 Fruitville Rd	377-2020
Baker & Wife	2157 Siesta Dr	960-1765
Bijou Cafe	1287 First St	366-8111
Blu Kouzina	25 N Blvd of Pres.	388-2619
Blu Que Island Grill	149 Avenida Messina	346-0738
Cafe Gabbiano	5104 Ocean Blvd	349-1423
Cafe L'Europe	431 St Armands Cir	388-4415
The Columbia	411 St Armands Cir	388-3987
Currents	1000 Blvd of the Arts	953-1234
Derek's Rustic Coastal	5516 Manatee Ave	794-1100
Drunken Poet Cafe	1572 Main St	955-8404
Duval's New World Cafe	1435 Main St	312-4001
Eat Here	240 Avenida Madera	346-7800
Euphemia Haye	5540 Gulf of Mexico Dr	383-3633
Fleming's Steakhouse	2001 Siesta Dr	358-9463

ONLINE RESERVATIONS		
Restaurant Name	**Address**	**Phone #**
Libby's Cafe + Bar	1917 Osprey Ave	487-7300
Louies Modern	1289 N Palm Ave	552-9688
Mattison's Forty One	7275 S Tamiami Trl	921-3400
Mediterraneo	1970 Main St	365-4122
Melange	1568 Main St	953-7111
Michael's On East	1212 East Ave	366-0007
Mozaic	1377 Main St	951-6272
Oh Mamma Mia!	2324 Gulf Gate Dr	706-2821
Ophelia's on the Bay	9105 Midnight Pass	349-2212
Pattigeorge's	7120 Gulf of Mexico Dr	383-5111
Pier 22	1200 1st Avenue W	748-8087
Polo Bar & Grill	10670 Boardwalk Lp	782-0899
Roast Restaurant & Bar	1296 First St	953-1971
Roy's Restaurant	2001 Siesta Dr	952-0109
Ruth's Chris Steakhouse	6700 S Tamiami Trl	942-9442
Salute! Ristorante	23 N Lemon Ave	365-1020
Selva Grill	1345 Main St	362-4427
EASY ON YOUR WALLET		
Anna Maria Oyster Bar	6906 14th St W	758-7880
Anna Maria Oyster Bar	6696 Cortez Rd	792-0077
Anna Maria Oyster Bar	1525 51st Ave E	721-7773
Coffee Carrousel	1644 Main St	365-2826
Casey Key Fish House	801 Blackburn Pt Rd	966-1901
Demetrio's Restaurant	4410 S Tamiami Trl	922-1585
El Toro Bravo	2720 Stickney Pt	924-0006
Gentile Cheesesteaks	7523 S Tamiami Trl	926-0441
Hob Nob Drive-In	1701 Washington Blvd	955-5001

EASY ON YOUR WALLET		
Restaurant Name	**Address**	**Phone #**
Hot Diggity Dog	5666 Swift Rd	922-8018
Il Panificio	1703 Main St	366-5570
Il Panificio	6630 Gateway Ave	921-5570
LeLu Coffee Lounge	5251 Ocean Blvd	346-5358
Main Bar Sandwich Shp	1944 Main St	955-8733
Mi Tierra Restaurant	1068 N Washington	330-0196
Michelle's Brown Bag	1819 Main St	365-5858
Mozzarella Fella	1668 Main St	366-7600
Munchies 420 Cafe	6639 Superior Ave	929-9393
New Pass Grill	1505 Ken Thompson	388-3119
3.14 Pi Craft Beer	5263 Ocean Blvd	346-1188
Pho Cali	1578 Main St	955-2683
Piccolo Italian Market	6518 Gateway Ave	923-2202
The Russian House	6115 S Tamiami Trl	735-1151
S'Macks Burgers	2407 Bee Ridge Rd	922-7673
Tasty Home Cookin'	3854 S Tuttle Ave	921-4969
Tony's Chicago Beef	6569 Superior Ave	922-7979
Yoder's Restaurant	3434 Bahia Vista	955-7771

NEW		
Adriatico	6606 Superior Ave	922-3080
Baker & Wife	2157 Siesta Dr	960-1765
Blu Kouzina	25 N Blvd of Pres.	388-2619
Curry Station	1303 N Washington	312-6264
Mandeville Beer Garden	428 N Lemon Ave	954-8688
Marcello's Ristorante	4155 S Tamiami Trl	921-6794
Muse At The Ringling	5401 Bay Shore Rd	360-7390

NEW		
Restaurant Name	**Address**	**Phone #**
3.14 Pi Craft Beer	5263 Ocean Blvd	346-1188
Pino's	3800 S Tamiami Trl	366-1440
Queen Of Sheba	34195 N Tamiami Trl	359-8000
Rosati's Pizza	935 N Beneva Rd	953-1802
Shaner's Pizza	6500 Superior Ave	927-2708
Sol Meyer's NY Deli	1473 Main St.	955-3354
Surf Shack	326 John Ringling Blvd	960-1122
Toasted Mango Cafe	6621 Midnight Pass	552-6485
Yo Sushi!	140 Univ. Town Ctr Dr	313-7091

SPORTS + FOOD + FUN		
Capt. Curt's Oyster Bar	1200 Old Stickney Pt	349-3885
Daiquiri Deck Raw Bar	5250 Ocean Blvd	349-8697
Gecko's Grill & Pub	4870 S Tamiami Trl	923-8896
Gecko's Grill & Pub	1900 Hillview St	953-2929
Gecko's Grill & Pub	5588 Palmer Crossing	923-6061
Miller's Ale House	3800 Kenny Dr	378-8888
The Old Salty Dog	5023 Ocean Blvd	349-0158
Sarasota Brewing Co	6607 Gateway Ave	925-2337
Siesta Key Oyster Bar	5238 Ocean Blvd	346-5443
GREAT BURGERS		
Baker & Wife	2157 Siesta Dr	960-1765
Gecko's Grill & Pub	4870 S Tamiami Trl	923-8896
Hillview Grill	1920 Hillview Ave	952-0045
Hob Nob Drive-In	1701 Washington Blvd	955-5001
Knick's Tavern & Grill	1818 S Osprey Ave	955-7761
Libby's Cafe + Bar	1917 Osprey Ave	487-7300

GREAT BURGERS		
Restaurant Name	**Address**	**Phone #**
MacAllisters Grill	8110 Lakewood Main	359-2424
Made	1990 Main St	953-2900
Mar-Vista Restaurant	760 Broadway St	383-2391
New Pass Grill	1505 Ken Thompson	388-3119
Old Packinghouse Cafe	987 S Packinghouse	371-9358
Patrick's 1481	1481 Main St	955-1481
Rev-el-ry Pub & Grill	3005 University Pkwy	355-1218
S'Macks Burgers	2407 Bee Ridge Rd	922-7673
Square 1 Burgers	1737 S Tamiami Trl	870-8111
Tasty Home Cookin'	3854 S Tuttle Ave	921-4969
Tony's Chicago Beef	6569 Superior Ave	922-7979

HELP MAKE A DIFFERENCE IN OUR SARASOTA-MANATEE COMMUNITY

Listed below are two local organizations that are striving to assist those in need in our Sarasota area. They could use your help. Please consider a donation to either (or both) during 2016.

ALL FAITHS FOOD BANK
WHAT THEY NEED: Donations of non-perishable, frozen and perishable food items needed. Monetary donations are also accepted and can be made directly through their website.
MORE INFO: www.allfaithsfoodbank.org

MAYORS FEED THE HUNGRY PROGRAM
WHAT THEY NEED: Donations of food, time and money are needed. This program hosts a large food drive in the month of November. Check their website for details or to make a monetary donation.
MORE INFO: mayorsfeedthehungry.org

NICE WINE LIST		
Restaurant Name	**Address**	**Phone #**
Adriatico	6606 Superior Ave	922-3080
Amore By Andrea	555 Bay Isles Pkwy	383-1111
15 South Ristorante	15 S Blvd of Pres.	708-8312
62 Bistrot	1962 Hillview St	954-1011
Andrea's	2085 Siesta Dr	951-9200
Antoine's Restaurant	5020 Fruitville Rd	377-2020
Beach Bistro	6600 Gulf Dr N	778-6444
BeachHouse Restaurant	200 Gulf Dr N	779-2222
Bijou Cafe	1287 First St	366-8111
Cafe Gabbiano	5104 Ocean Blvd	349-1423
Cafe L'Europe	431 St Armands Cir	388-4415
Currents	1000 Blvd of the Arts	953-1234
Derek's Rustic Coastal	5516 Manatee Ave	794-1100
Dolce Italia	6606 Superior Ave	921-7007
Duval's New World Cafe	1435 Main St	312-4001
Euphemia Haye	5540 Gulf of Mexico Dr	383-3633
Flavio's Brick Oven	5239 Ocean Blvd	349-0995
Fleming's Steakhouse	2001 Siesta Dr	358-9463
Harry's Continental Kit.	525 St Judes Dr	383-0777
Hyde Park Steakhouse	35 S Lemon Ave	366-7781
Indigenous	239 Links Ave	706-4740
Libby's Cafe + Bar	1917 Osprey Ave	487-7300
Lido Beach Grille	700 Ben Franklin Dr	388-2161
Louies Modern	1289 N Palm Ave	552-9688
Maison Blanche	2605 Gulf of Mexico Dr	383-8088
Marcello's Ristorante	4155 S Tamiami Trl	921-6794
Mattison's Forty One	7275 S Tamiami Trl	921-3400

NICE WINE LIST		
Restaurant Name	**Address**	**Phone #**
Mattison's Forty One	7275 S Tamiami Trl	921-3400
Michael's On East	1212 East Ave	366-0007
Miguel's	6631 Midnight Pass	349-4024
Mozaic	1377 Main St	951-6272
Ophelia's on the Bay	9105 Midnight Pass	349-2212
Ortygia	1418 13th Street W	741-8646
Pattigeorge's	7120 Gulf of Mexico Dr	383-5111
Pier 22	1200 1st Avenue W	748-8087
Polo Bar & Grill	10670 Boardwalk Lp	782-0899
Pomona Bistro	481 N Orange Ave	706-1677
Roast Restaurant & Bar	1296 First St	953-1971
Roessler's	2033 Vamo Way	966-5688
Rosebud's Steakhouse	2215 S Tamiami Trl	918-8771
Ruth's Chris Steakhouse	6700 S Tamiami Trl	942-9442
Salute! Ristorante	23 N Lemon Ave	365-1020
Sardinia	5770 S Tamiami Trl	702-8582
Selva Grill	1345 Main St	362-4427
Solorzano's	6516 Superior Ave	906-9444
The Table Creekside	5365 S Tamiami Trl	921-9465
Treviso	5401 Bay Shore Rd	360-7390
Waterfront	7660 S Tamiami Trl	921-1916

A BEAUTIFUL WATER VIEW		
Beach Bistro	6600 Gulf Dr N	778-6444
BeachHouse Restaurant	200 Gulf Dr N	779-2222
Boatyard Waterfront Grill	1500 Stickney Pt Rd	921-6200
Casey Key Fish House	801 Blackburn Pt Rd	966-1901

A BEAUTIFUL WATER VIEW		
Restaurant Name	**Address**	**Phone #**
The Crow's Nest	1968 Tarpon Ctr Dr	484-9551
Dry Dock Waterfront	412 Gulf of Mexico Dr	383-0102
Jack Dusty	1111 Ritz-Carlton Dr	309-2266
Lido Beach Grille	700 Ben Franklin Dr	388-2161
Marina Jack's	2 Marina Plaza	365-4243
Mar-Vista Restaurant	760 Broadway St	383-2391
New Pass Grill	1505 Ken Thompson	388-3119
Ophelia's on the Bay	9105 Midnight Pass	349-2212
Pattigeorge's	7120 Gulf of Mexico Dr	383-5111
Phillippi Creek Oyster	5363 S Tamiami Trl	925-4444
Pier 22	1200 1st Avenue W	748-8087
Riverhouse Reef Grill	995 Riverside Dr	729-0616
The Sandbar	100 Spring Ave	778-0444
Sharkey's on the Pier	1600 Harbor Dr S	488-1456
The Table Creekside	5365 S Tamiami Trl	921-9465
Turtle's	8875 Midnight Pass	346-2207
Waterfront	7660 S Tamiami Trl	921-1916

LATER NIGHT MENU		
15 South Ristorante	15 S Blvd of Pres.	708-8312
Blase Cafe	5263 Ocean Blvd	349-9822
Blu Que Island Grill	149 Avenida Messina	346-0738
Blue Rooster	1524 4th St	388-7539
Cafe Epicure	1298 Main St	366-5648
Capt. Curt's Oyster Bar	1200 Old Stickney Pt	349-3885
Clasico Cafe + Bar	1341 Main St	957-0700
The Cottage	153 Avenida Messina	312-9300
Daiquiri Deck Raw Bar	5250 Ocean Blvd	349-8697

LATER NIGHT MENU		
Restaurant Name	Address	Phone #
Flavio's Brick Oven	5239 Ocean Blvd	349-0995
Gecko's Grill & Pub	4870 S Tamiami Trl	923-8896
Gecko's Grill & Pub	1900 Hillview St	953-2929
Gilligan's Island Bar	5253 Ocean Blvd	346-8122
Heaven Ham/Devil Dogs	2647 Mall Dr	923-2514
Knick's Tavern & Grill	1818 S Osprey Ave	955-7761
Louies Modern	1289 N Palm Ave	552-9688
Lynches Pub & Grub	19 N Blvd of Pres	388-5550
Made	1990 Main St	953-2900
Mandeville Beer Garden	428 N Lemon Ave	954-8688
Marina Jack's	2 Marina Plaza	365-4243
Mattison's City Grille	1 N Lemon Ave	330-0440
Miller's Ale House	3800 Kenny Dr	378-8888
Munchies 420 Cafe	6639 Superior Ave	929-9393
3.14 Pi Craft Beer	5263 Ocean Blvd	346-1188
Patrick's 1481	1481 Main St	955-1481
Phillippi Creek Oyster	5363 S Tamiami Trl	925-4444
Pub 32	8383 S Tamiami Trl	952-3070
Sarasota Brewing Co	6607 Gateway Ave	925-2337
Sharkey's on the Pier	1600 Harbor Dr S	488-1456
Siesta Key Oyster Bar	5238 Ocean Blvd	346-5443
Social Eatery & Bar	1219 First St	444-7072
State St Eating House	1533 State St	951-1533
The Starlite Room	1001 Cocoanut Ave	702-5613
Two Senorita's	1355 Main St	366-1618
Walt's Fish Market	4144 S Tamiami Trl	921-4605
Yume Sushi	1532 Main St	363-0604

PIZZA PIE!		
Restaurant Name	**Address**	**Phone #**
Cafe Don Giovanni	5610 Gulf of Mexico Dr	383-0013
Cafe Epicure	1298 Main St	366-5648
Caragiulos	69 S Palm Ave	951-0866
Cosimo's Trattoria	3501 Palmer Crossing	922-7999
Demetrio's Restaurant	4410 S Tamiami Trl	922-1585
Eat Here	240 Avenida Madera	346-7800
Flavio's Brick Oven	5239 Ocean Blvd	349-0995
Il Panificio	1703 Main St	366-5570
Il Panificio	6630 Gateway Ave	921-5570
Joey D's Chicago Eatery	3811 Kenny Dr	376-8900
Main Street Trattoria	8131 Lakewood Main	907-1518
Mattison's City Grille	1 N Lemon Ave	330-0440
Matto Matto	543 S Pineapple Ave	951-2600
Mediterraneo	1970 Main St	365-4122
3.14 Pi Craft Beer	5263 Ocean Blvd	346-1188
Primo! Ristorante	8076 N Tamiami Trl	359-3690
Rosati's Pizza	935 N Beneva Rd	953-1802
Sarasota Brewing Co	6607 Gateway Ave	925-2337
Shaner's Pizza	6500 Superior Ave	927-2708
Solorzano Bros. Pizza	3604 Webber St	926-4276
Solorzano Bros. Pizza	5251 Ocean Blvd	346-5358

SARASOTA FINE DINING		
Andrea's	2085 Siesta Dr	951-9200
Beach Bistro	6600 Gulf Dr N	778-6444
Bijou Cafe	1287 First St	366-8111
Derek's Rustic Coastal	5516 Manatee Ave	794-1100